A SIMPLE GUIDE TO
SUFISM

Farida Khanam

GOODWORD
www.goodwordbooks.com

Contents

1. Sufism ... 7

2. Origin and Historical Development of History ... 9

3. Gradual Evolution of Tasawwuf ... 20

4. Chishti Order-1 ... 29

5. Chishti Order-2 ... 45

6. Chishti Order-3 ... 60

7. Qadiri Order ... 70

8. Suhrawardi Order ... 89

9. Naqshbandi Order-1 ... 108

10. Naqshbandi Order-2 ... 119

11. Naqshbandi Order-3 ... 129

12. Firdausi Order ... 141

13. The Sufi Concept of Meditation ... 154

Sufism

What is Sufism?

SUFISM *(TASAWWUF)* IS the form which mysticism has taken in Islam. The term Sufism embraces the philosophy and practices in Islam which aim at direct communion between God and man.

The Derivation of Sufi

SCHOLARS DIFFER AS to the meaning and derivation of this word which is used for those who opt for this spiritual path. Some of them associate it with the Arabic word 'safa' meaning purity. Others are of the view that it may refer to the Ashabus Safa, or the people of the bench. When the Prophet migrated to Madinah, with his companions, the majority of them managed to earn their livelihood by engaging in trade or taking up some employment. Some of them worked in orchards, while others engaged in trade as they used to do in Makkah. But there were a sizeable number of people who could not engage themselves in any such activity. They did not even have their own roof to take shelter under. These people used to stay in the verandah or porch of the Prophet's mosque. Here they spent their time in worship, in listening to the Prophet's words and memorizing them. Similarly, they memorized the verses of the Quran as they were being revealed from time to time. Having all the time at their disposal, they managed to preserve in their memory, both the Quran and the Hadith.

Abu Hurayrah, being one of them, had memorized the greatest number of traditions. Having no worldly activities to engage their attention they lived a very simple life.

They often gathered sticks for a living and satisfied their hunger by eating the dates which had fallen from the palm trees.

The Prophet looked after them and asked his companions to help them. Since the porch of the mosque had become virtually their home, they came to be called Ashaabus Safa.

However, the majority of the scholars are of the opinion that the word sufi comes from the word 'Suf' or wool.

This is because most of the early ascetics wore undyed woolen garments of a coarse quality. This coarse cloth symbolized their voluntary poverty and renunciation of the world and all its pleasures.

Origin and Historical Development of History

The Beginnings of Sufism

THE SUFIS TRACE the origin of *Trasawwuf* to the Prophet of Islam himself. All the religious orders trace their lines of succession back to him. It is believed that the revelations received by the Prophet were two-dimensional—one was in the form of the words of the Quran, the other was in the form of divine inspiration within his heart. The former was meant for all, while the latter was to be imparted to the chosen few through a line of succession, that is from heart to heart. "Book knowledge". — of the words of the Quran and Hadith — was known as *ilm-e-Safina*, while "heart-knowledge" was known as *ilm-e-Sina*.

The knowledge of the wonders of the Quran and Hadith was passed on from one generation to another by the religious scholars or *Ulama* while the knowledge of the heart was imbibed by those called Sufis.

The claim of the Sufis that *tasawwuf* originated from the life of the Prophet and his companions seems to have some basis in fact. The Prophet led an extremely simple life. He avoided all luxuries. He would pray to God for a major portion of the night (Quran 73:20) whatever valuable presents he received he immediately disposed of in charity. Even when he had conquered Arabia, he did not possess more than an ordinary mattress to sleep on and a pitcher to keep water in. He fasted continuously for months together and slept little at night.

Thus the Prophet committed himself to religion in both theory and practice at a deeper level.

There are also traditions which tell us that the Prophet discouraged people from spending all their time in ritual worship and not taking interest in worldly activities.

Sufis have always laid emphasis on Safa, that is, purification. The Quran has this to say: He indeed shall be successful who purifies himself. (87:14) He will indeed be successful who purifies his soul, and he will indeed fail who corrupts his soul. (91:9-10)

We learn from the Quran that God made the human soul perfect and inspired it to understand what is right and wrong for it. (91:7,8) So the purification of the heart and soul is essential to attain divine appoval.

There comes a stage where man's will becomes one with the divine will. And there is the type of man who gives his life to seek the pleasure of God. And God is full of kindness to his servants. (2:207)

The Rite of Purification

SACRIFICING ONE'S LIFE for God is the only way to win Divine approval. The rite of unification is essential for the follower of the spiritual path.

In Sufism, the follower, the Salik receives the rite of initiation from his Shaykh or Murshid, who in his turn has received it from his Shaykh and this chain goes back to the Prophet himself.

They believe that the Prophet conferred this right upon only some of his companions, who in turn passed it on to their companions and in this way this right up to the present day in unbroken succession is still passed on. This chain of succession is known in Arabic as *silsilah*. The mystic was first a seeker, then a traveller and then an initiate.

For the achievement of spiritual realization, the initiation, the counsel, and guidance of the Shaykh, or spiritual master, is necessary.

It is around the Shaykh that the disciples gather to receive the initiation which, through a long chain is ultimately derived from the Prophet himself as the Sufis believe. All the *silsilahs* are traced back to one or the other of those companions whom the Prophet himself initiated. Particularly the caliphs Abu Bakr and Ali.

The first great Sufi order was the Qadri order (*Tariqa*) which was founded by Shaykh Abdul Qadir Jilani (1071-1166).

This was followed by the Suhrawardi Order (1144-1234).

There are three great categories of the religion of Islam: *Iman*: Submission to the revealed law, *Itaah*: obedience to the *Shahaadah* (The Islamic Creed), and *Ihsan*: Virtue and sincerity.

A tradition regarding *Ihsaan* as narrated by Caliph Umar, reads, "One day when we were with the Prophet of God, there came to him a man whose clothes were of an exceeding whiteness, and his hair was of an exceeding blackness, nor were there any signs of travel upon him. Although none of us had seen him before, he sat down opposite the Prophet. He asked the Prophet to tell him what it means to surrender to God. The Prophet answered: "The surrender is that you should say five prayers, fast during Ramadan, distribute alms and, if you can, go on the pilgrimage to the Holy house (the Kabah)." He said: "You have spoken truly." We were amazed that, having questioned the Prophet, he should corroborate what he said.

Then he said: Tell me what faith (*Iman*) is. Then the Prophet said: "It is that you should believe in God, in angels and the books, the prophets and the Last Day, and you should believe that no good or evil comes but by His providence." "You have spoken truly," he said, and then he said, "Tell me what excellence, *Ihsan* is." The Prophet answered, "It is that you should worship God as if you saw Him, or if you do not see Him, truly, He sees you." Then the stranger went away. I (Umar) stayed there long after he had gone, until the Prophet said to him, "O Umar, do you know who the questioner was?" I said "God and His Prophet know best, but I do not know at all." "It was Gabriel," said the Prophet. "He came to teach you your religion." This spiritual way emphasizes the inner illumination of Islam and *Imaan* by *Ihsan*. *Dhikr*: Remembrance of God, is necessary to achieve excellence (*Ihsaan*). In this spiritual path *dhikr* is of the utmost importance.

The recitation of a special Quranic *litany* (*Wird*) is an important sufi practice. It differs slightly from one order to another. First the Salik asks forgiveness from God. Second, he asks God to bless the Prophet, the third formula comprises the Shahadah, the attestation of the divine Unity.

The rosary is normally recited morning and evening. Each formula being repeated a hundred times. Dhikr means remembrance of God. It is most important so far as the spiritual method of the Sufis is concerned. The Quran attaches the utmost importance to the remembrance of God, by invoking His name. "Invoke the name of your Lord and devote yourself to Him with utter devotion." (73:8).

Prayer preserves one from uncleanness and grave sin, but "remembrance of God is greatest." (29:45)

Verily in the remembrance of God do hearts finds rest.

"Remember Me and I shall remember You. (2:152).

In Sufism *Dhikr* has the central place in the spiritual method. The Sufi has to practice it under the guidance of a Spiritual master. *Dhikr* is done in both gatherings and in spiritual retrial privacy (*Khalwat*).

In most orders, formal *dhikr* sessions (*Majaalis*) are held at regular intervals. Under the guidance of his Shaykh or his representative, the *Salik* (disciple) engages in *Dhikr* for an hour or two. This may be done silently or loudly in the form of a chant, motionlessly or accompanied by spiritual music and dance. At times, the music is accompanied by the beatings of a drum. *Khalwat* (Solitary spiritual retreat) for the purpose of spiritual invocation is engaged in from time to time. This may go on for as short a period as several hours or may last several days. Along with this, *Dhikr* is to be done silently at all times of the day, even when one is engaged in other activities.

Objectives

THERE ARE DIFFERENT levels of excellence of worship. The objective of *tasawwuf* is to raise this level. It is called '*Ihsan*' in the Quran.

Ihsaan is the level at which the devotee is completely absorbed in prayer to God. According to a hadith, you should pray to God as if you saw Him. And if you can't see Him, He sees you.*

Ihsan is defined by Sufis, as the attainment of that degree of devotion at which one begins to experience the presence of God one's feelings ranging back and forth between hope and fear. The Quran lays down that the path of virtue lies between hope and fear. It is very clear on this point when it says: "And pray to Him with fear and hope; His mercy is within reach of the righteous." (7:55).

Thus, according to the Sufi definition, consciousness of the fact that the Lord is watching our movements and knows the innermost recesses of our hearts is the lowest grade of devotion and prayer. When one is conscious of the fact that God is watching us, then we certainly shall desist from evil actions. It is in this sense that prayer keeps us from indecency and evil, as is stated in the Quran. (29:45).

However, it is only if the prayer is performed in its true spirit that it can yield the desired result. This is the first grade level of piety: God is watching us. On the second level we are seeing God. When one, loving God, with his whole heart prostrates himself and at other moments when he has the

---

*Al-Bukhari Sahih, Kitab al Iman.

psychological experience of seeing God face to face, his total absorption results in ecstasy. So the Sufis say.

They have the feeling of seeing God, their beloved One, as they call Him. There are even instances of Sufis having fallen senseless when possessed by the manifestations of extreme love. The Sufis say that the Prophet and some of his companions were totally absorbed in their prayers and that this complete absorption in prayer is the foundation of ecstasy.

The Sufis hold that at the time of the Prophet and his companions, the obligatory prayers were done with full concentration in complete remembrance of God. But later on, the Sufis emphasized *Dhikr* to the point that it was given more importance than even the canonical prayers.

Dhikr literally means remembering God. The Quran Says "Remember God always so that you may prosper." (62:10) Then at another place, it says: "Believers, be ever mindful of God: praise Him morning and evening." (33:41).

The Quran mentions 99 different names of God and according to another version God has as many as 90,000 names. Each name indicates a particular attribute of God.

So the believers used to remember God even when performing their worldly duties. They believed that they would also receive a reward for discharging their duties to their fellow men, while still remembering God and acting in accordance with His will. The idea was that anything done in the name of God, conforming to His commands amounted to remembering God or performing *Dhikr*.

And it is, in this sense that the Prophet's companions understood the meaning of *Dhikr*, that is, remembering God even when they were performing worldly duties. But the Sufis gave *Dhikr* a formal shape, attaching greater importance to its popular meaning. In this way, they limited the scope of this verse of the Quran. And giving subsidence to this limited interpretation, the Sufis invented a number of ways of calling out the name of God—silently loudly and even with the beating of drums. This shows how much the teachings of Islam came under the influence of different cultures.

Besides, converts from different traditions brought their own influences from their own cultures and gradually they were all Islamized, or given Islamic names, Such as the yogic practices which found acceptance among the Sufis.

The Prophet's companions and the Companions of the Companions regarded all forms of prayers other than compulsory prayers as *Nawafils* or works of supererogation; In Islam this term was used in the sense of doing good in addition to the performance of one's obligatory duties (*Faraiz*) Islam enjoins a minimum of duties to be discharged by the believers and this is given the name of *Faraid*. Anyone who enters the fold of Islam has to discharge these minimal duties, but if he does more than this then he doubly earns the favour of All-Merciful God by his additional acts. This is known as *Nafl*. The Prophet himself used to perform supererogatory prayers. He used to say his midnight prayers but he and his followers interpreted nafl in a very general sense and understood from it, good actions performed over and above one's duties. The later Sufis, however, restricted the word to its narrow sense of saying prayers in addition to the fixed prayers. They did the same to limit the meaning of the word *Dhikr* to only repeating the names of God. This change took place so slowly that proper notice could not be taken in time and these notions came to be accepted by the general public. Another thing, which was not in accordance with the spirit of the Quran was that the Sufis attached too great an importance to the mere recitation chanting of the words of the Quran. In the true Islamic spirit, it is not the mere recitation of the words which is important, but rather the spirit of prayer, and our attachment to God, and our willingness to surrender our will to His will, by perusing and reflecting upon the meanings of the divine words. Now, if we are perpetually confined to a *Hujra* (a small, dark room) for worship, how can we be tested on whether or not we have surrendered to God's will in our day-to-day life.

God has made this world a testing ground. And the divine test can be carried out only when we interact with others, when we have dealings with others, and we always act with thoughts of God in our minds. So, it is in our discharging of our worldly duties that we are tested on whether or not we have truly imbibed the True Islamic Spirit.

God has not told us to worship Him, in the formal sense, twenty four hours a day. Therefore, if we follow this path, it would amount to a shift in emphasis. According to the Quran, God desires us that He be eternally remembered, while taking part in all the lawful activities of the world.

So the great importance given to the chanting of certain words and phrases for long hours amount to a shift of emphasis. In the Indian context, the Sufis definitely came under the influence of Yogi Spiritual Exercises. In Hinduism, it was believed that words had special effect and that by chanting them, a certain number of times, even gods could be controlled, and their favours could be received.

The early Sufis laid stress, above all on the renunciation of worldly pleasures. And they also emphasized the fear of God and Judgement Day and that their thoughts should be centered on the fact that we will be judged according to our good and bad deeds on the Day of Judgement. So we have the early celebrated Sufis like Hasan Basri, Abn Darda who used to remember God most of the time; they would pray to God, and cry to seek His pardon. When asked why they did so, they would reply that even if they had not made any intentional mistake, they might have made some unintentional mistake. So they kept seeking God's forgiveness and for the greater part they would resort to Nafl prayer, remembering God, reciting the verses of the Quran and always going in fear of God. Their most characteristic feature was that they did not want to involve themselves in the world. This is the point of departure from the spirituality of the Companions of the Prophet.

For we find that in the life and times of the Prophet, he and his companions and their companions performed all their worldly duties and in doing so, they remembered God and they thought that if they did all those necessary mundane activities and in the midst of that, they continued to remember God and their thoughts were centered on God, they would earn a double reward—one for discharging the obligatory duties and the other for remembering God at times other than those of formal worship.

The early Sufis became known for their asceticism. Poverty was their ideal. They thought that it was the world which distracted their attention. So, if they did not accumulate worldly things, they would be spared any distraction so their prayers would become of a far better quality, because of their full concentration.

Gradual Evolution of Tasawwuf

The Early Sufis

RENUNCIATION OF THE world and an intense fear of God was the outstanding feature of this discipline as practiced by the early Sufis. It was much later that foreign elements crept into it, in particular the concept of pantheism. Thus the early Sufis were ascetics in the true sense of the word. Poverty was their ideal. They believed that wealth and other worldly goods presented an obstruction and a distraction from leading a proper religious life. They believed that the desired concentration is possible only when we free ourselves from worldly desires. Only then can we fully devote ourselves to the path of earning divine pleasure. For, when even in worldly matters full dedication and devotion are required to achieve worldly success, how can one succeed in the next eternal life without total devotion and dedication?

Ibn Khaldun has aptly summed up the way of life of the early Sufis: The way of the Sufis was regarded by the early Muslims as the way of Truth and salvation. They zealously guarded the piety, gave up everything for God's sake achieved all objects of worldly attraction, renounced pleasure, wealth and power, abandoned society and lead a life in seclusion devoted to the service of God. These were the fundamental principles of Sufism which prevailed among the companions and Muslims of the early times.

Thus we find that the first phase of Sufism was a form of asceticism. This lifestyle based on asceticism was in fact the direct consequence of the Islamic concept of God.

There are a number of traditions which tell us how the companions of the Prophet and the companions' companions went in awe and fear of God. Hasan Basri, the celebrated Sufi of the first phase had once told his disciples: I have seen people among the Prophet's companions to whom the world meant less than the dust under their feet. Hasan Basri had met a large number of the companions of the Prophet, including seventy senior companions. Hasan Basri also told of how they wore simple, homespun Camel hair garments, and were so preoccupied with righteous living that they seemed lost to the world. "Were they to see the best among you, they would think: "These people do not believe in the Day of Judgement."" So the hallmark of the Companions and their disciples was their deep consciousness of the sin of disobedience and extreme dread of divine punishment. They often passed the whole night in vigil, repeating the verse of the Quran. (45:20)

Rabia Basri (d. 801) once observed "the love of God has so absorbed me that neither love nor hate of any other thing remains in my heart."

Abu Darda, a senior companion of the Prophet used to

say: If you knew what you shall see after death, you would not eat food nor drink water with any relish; as for myself I wish that I were a tree which is chopped and then devoured."

Abu Bakr, the first caliph, seeing a bird sitting on a tree, exclaimed, "Oh bird, how fortunate you are. If only I could be like you sitting on trees, eating their fruit and then flying away. No reckoning or doom awaits you. By God, I would like to be a tree by the wayside, and have a passing camel take me in its mouth, chew me, swallow me and then dispose of me as dung." *(Al-Baihaqi, Al Sunan Al-Kabra)*

Abu Darda, a senior companion of the Prophet, was once told that Abu Saad ibn Munabbih had freed a hundred slaves. His comment was: Certainly this is a great act. But let me tell you of one that is even greater: faith which encompasses night and day, and, on one's tongue, the constant remembrance of God." (Hilyat al-Auliya)

When Abu Darda died, someone asked his wife what the nature of her late husband's worship had been. "He used to spend the whole day also, engrossed in thought," She told him (Hilyat al-auliya).

There is a hadith to this effect reported by Abu Darda: The Prophet once asked his companions: "Should I not tell you of the action that is best and most pure in the presence of your Lord; the action which will raise you up in the sight of God, and is better for you than great expenditure of gold and silver (in charity)?" Do tell us", the companions replied, "It is the remembrance of God," Said the Prophet (Al-Tirmidhi, Shamail)

Oppressive circumstances during the Umayyad rule were

a further reason for the Sufis opting for a life of asceticism. The Ummayyad caliphs had deviated from the path followed by the four pious caliphs preceding them. They preferred a life of luxury as opposed to the life of extreme simplicity of the pious caliphs. The Shariah was bypassed at will. The Umayyads discriminated between their tribesmen, their supporters and those who did not support their unjust policies. They put undue pressure upon the governors, the Qazis (judges). The governors in their turn took oppressive measures against those who did not support their unjust policies.

Since the people felt themselves helpless to counter the oppressive rule, they turned inwards, withdrawing from the world itself.

Hasan al-Basri (642-728) is the most prominent name in this early ascetic movement. He was born in Madinah and he settled in Basra. He was famous for his learning. A large number of students came to seek knowledge from him. Once he observed: "This world is a bridge which you cross but upon which you should not build."

Therefore, the pious Muslims did not want to associate themselves with the rulers and be a part of the government machinery. Hence, they withdrew from the world to lead a life of devotion and worship of God in seclusion.

It is said that fear of God seized him so greatly that it seemed as though hellfire had been created for him alone. It is said that one day a friend saw him weeping and asked him the reason. He replied that, he was weeping for fear that he might have done something wrong unintentionally, or committed some fault or spoken some word which was unpleasing to God, then He may have said, 'Begone, for you have no more favour with Me."

Rabia Basri (713-801) was one of the most famous saints in Islam in its early phase. She was born, lived and died in Basra. She belonged to a poor family, and during a famine she was sold into slavery. She used to worship God in any spare time she had from her duties as a slave. Finally her master, seeing her inclinations, set her free. From then on, she devoted all her time to worshipping God Almighty. She lived a life of extreme asceticism. Her mystical sayings have become proverbs. She developed the concept of 'Divine Love' and intimacy with God.

Rabia followed the path of *Tawakkul,* — resignation and dependence on God. She lived a life of extreme poverty. Whenever anyone wanted to help her, she replied: I should be ashamed to ask for worldly things from Him to whom the world belongs; how, then should I ask for them from those to whom it does not belong."

Rabia Basri's greatest contribution to Islamic Sufism was to develop the conception of prayer as free and intimate intercourse with God. Prayer, for her was not just a means of avoiding hell and of gaining paradise, but they were to her the means of gaining access to God's Presence. Her prayers were a spontaneous outpouring of her heart to God.

She held that God should be loved and worshipped, without any consideration of selfish ends. She criticized those who worshipped God to secure His favours. Once she observed: I want to light a fire in Paradise and pour water in hell so that people no longer worship God for hope of Paradise and for fear of hell.

She wanted God to be worshipped for the sake of the love of God alone and not for any selfish ends. One of her prayers is as follows:

"O my Lord, If I worship You from fear of Hell, burn me in Hell, and if I worship, You out of hope of Paradise, exclude me from it, but if I worship You for Your own sake, then with hold not from me, Your eternal beauty."

By the time of Hasan Basri and Rabia Basri, asceticism was the main feature of Islamic Sufism. The Sufis wanted to withdraw from the world and devoted all their time to worshipping God. To focus their attention on this spiritual path, it was essential for them to keep themselves away from the world. This was possible only by limiting their necessities, leading a life to the bare minimum. All the time they had at their disposal was spent in performing supererogatory prayers, fasting, etc. They took extra care that all their time was spent in the remembrance of God in all sincerity.

In this, they had departed very little from the path of earning God's pleasure shown by the Quran and Hadith.

The point of departure between a Sufi-believer and a non-Sufi believer was that the Sufi believed in retiring from the world and spending all their time in the worship of God, while the stand of the non-Sufi believers was that, after performing obligatory forms of worship, they must engage themselves in other social duties as well. And if these duties were performed in accordance with the will of God, they would be rewarded by God for this just as they were rewarded for His worship.

The early Sufis believed that the fewer the worldly

possessions, the more they would be able to devote themselves selflessly to the worship of God. Thus, having fewer goods was taken as a guarantee to secure an entry into paradise. That is the reason why poverty was held as an ideal by these Sufis.

Then came the stage of believing that just having no wealth in one's possession was not enough. Rather one's heart should be free from any such desire. Thus, the hand as well as the heart should be empty to attain the desired result. This lack of desire was regarded as 'true poverty'. From the Sufis point of view, complete detachment from all finite things was essential. To this concept: Hazrat Nizamuddin Auliya gives an ancient expression:

"Rejection of the world does not mean that one should strip oneself of one's clothes and sit idle. Rejection of the world means that one may put on clothes and take food. But one should not set one's heart on anything. This and this alone is rejection of the world."

However, we should not lose sight of the fact that these early Sufis were all practicing Muslims in that they observed all the obligatory form of worship. We may call them orthodox Muslims as far as their beliefs and practices are concerned. But in actual fact, they laid such great emphasis on certain points in the teachings of the Quran and Traditions that it almost amounted to a shift of emphasis. Gradually, Nawafil voluntary forms of worship came to be have more importance attached to it then the obligatory forms of worship.

At this stage, the Sufis were concerned only with matters having a bearing on practical theology. Metaphysical and theosophical speculations had not yet been introduced into this discipline.

Ibrahim ibn Adham (d. 783) Fudayl bin Ayadh (d. 801) and Rabia al Adwiyya are the most prominent Sufis of this period.

Ibrahim ibn Adham was of a princely family of Balkh. One day when he had gone out on a hunting expedition, he followed an antelope so far that he lost his way back home.

In this trying situation, he heard a strange voice which cried: "*Awake!* Were you created for this"? He was so moved by these words that he started thinking deeply about them. Finally, he came to the conclusion that his way of life was not accordance with the will of the Lord. He resolved to renounce his sinful ways. After spending a whole night in meditation, he repented and asked God to forgive him for leading such a neglectful life. From then on, he abandoned everything and entered upon the path of ascesiasm and piety.

One of his sayings is as follows:

"O God, you know that in my eyes paradise weighs no more than the wing of a gnat compared with that honour which you have shown me in giving me Your love, or that familiarity which You have given to me by the remembrance of Your name, or that freedom from all else which You have vouchsafed to me when I meditate on the greatness of Your glory."

The Lord answered his prayers. The next morning he was transformed. He renounced all his possessions and became a desciple of Abdul Wahid b. Zayd, a successor of Hasan Basri.

Ibrahim b. Adham achieved great heights in this path.

---

*Prof. Nicholson, a Literary History of the Arabs, p. 232.

He attached the maximum importance to the renunciation of the world, and to celibacy. He held that a true sufi is one who covets nothing of this world, nothing of the next, and denotes himself entirely to God.* Furthermore, he once observed: "he had left the world to the seekers of the world and the hereafter to the seekers of the hereafter. For himself, he had chosen the remembrance of God in this world and the beautific vision in the next."

He believed that the stages of true asceticism cannot be arrived at without the virtues of celibacy and poverty. Very intererestingly, he once remarked that when a sufi marries, it is for him like boarding a ship, but when a child is born to him his ship sinks and his asceticism disappears.

---

*Ali Huwari, Kashal Mahjoob, English translation by R.N.Nicholson, p. 217.

Chishti Order-1

THE CHISHTI ORDER originated in the town of Chisht in Khurasan, about one hundred kilometres to the east of Herat in Afghanistan. It was founded by Khwaja Abu Ishaq Shami Chishti, who came from Asia Minor and settled in Chist. He is believed to be the ninth after Ali in the line of spiritual succession. He was a disciple and Khalifa of Mimshad Dinwari, (the latter being a Khalifa of Hubayra of Basra and also a disciple of Junayd of Baghdad). The spiritual origin of this order was traced by the Shaykh back to Hazrat Ali and the Prophet Muhammad, and then through Hasan Basri.

The notable Sufis in this order were: Fudhail ibn Iyaz, Ibrahim Adham Balkhi Khwaja Mamshad and Khwaja Mawdud.

Khwaja Muinuddin Chishti, fourth in the line of succession after Khwaja Mawdud Chishti, popularised this order in India. He was born in about 1141-42 in Sijistan (Sistan) and was only fifteen years old when his father died. He inherited a garden and a water mill. After his father's death, the economic condition of his family having deteriorated, he himself used to work in the garden. One day while he was at work, a *majzub* (ecstatic) named Ibrahim Qanduzi came into his garden. The Khwaja, although just 15 year old, was very polite and cultured. He not only offered this dervish a seat under the trees, but he also brought him a bunch of grapes to eat. The dervish realized the spiritual potential in this boy. It is recorded that he took some sesame seeds out of his bag, chewed them and put them in Muinuddin's mouth. After his eating these seeds, a spiritual connection was established, and Muinuddin's potential spirituality was awakened. This experience revolutionized his thinking. Soon thereafter, Muinuddin sold his possessions and distributed the money among the poor.

This version of his decision to renounce the world is considered to be the most authentic. The shock of the untimely death of his father may have produced his introspective temperament, sincerity, seriousness, and the urge to devote his life to some higher purpose. Perhaps it was just such a jolt which was needed to take one who was immersed in the world away from all that was mundane and bring him into the realms of the spiritual. And it may well have been the visit of Khwaja Ibrahim which spurred him finally to detach his mind and heart from the world, so that he might devote himself to the spiritual life which he had been seeking all along.

Now he left his home and started moving from one place to another. He spent most of his time acquiring a knowledge of the Quran, Hadith, *fiqh* and theology. During these travels he met his spiritual guide, Shaykh Usman Harwani, a Sufi. For about two and a half years he practiced rigorous spiritual exercises. After completing his spiritual training to his mentor's complete satisfaction, he was given a *khirqa* (gown) by the Shaykh and appointed as his Khalifa. After this the Khwaja was allowed to impart spiritual training to his disciples.

He then left for Harwan, a suburb of Nishapur. During his journey he met a number of Shaykhs and received spiritual training from them. He also stayed with Shaykh Abdul Qadir Jilani for about two months. He continued to travel in this way for several years, meeting a number of celebrated Sufis on his way.

How interesting it is that in mediaeval times one could travel across almost the entire inhabited world without encountering any difficulties. This was fortunate, for in the Sufi tradition it was very important to undertake journeys in order to share the learning and experiences of other saints. This was, of course, a priority for Khwaja Muinuddin who, in the course of his long journey across Asia, right from Baghdad to Delhi, had the opportunity to meet great souls from whom he derived immense benefit. By the time he reached India, it had been conquered by Muslims, and northern India was under the rule of Qutbuddin Aibak, the representative of Mohd Ghauri.

Khwaja Muinuddin was a great humanitarian and well-wisher of his fellow men, so people thronged around him wherever he went. He truly cared not only for their spiritual uplift, but also for their physical well-being.

Because of this crowd of followers. he was left with little time for his spiritual devotions. So he decided to leave Delhi for Ajmer. By this time Ajmer had become quite a fertile ground in which to disseminate his teachings among the people, for not only the lower classes, but also a number of people from the upper classes had already converted to Islam.

Besides, another possible reason for choosing Ajmer as his centre of spiritual activity was that it was a remote place, away from intense political activity. In doing so, he was following the traditions laid down by the founders of the Chishti Silsila.

Khwaja Muinuddin's simple, ascetic life attracted both the Muslims and the Hindus. Both the conqueror and the conquered were reminded of the social and moral values of religion, which were universal in nature. The Khwaja did not attach importance to material power and wealth. He laid stress only on piety, simplicity, lawful earning, devotion to God and service to man. This appealed to all Hindus and Muslims, rich and poor, high and low, as these were addressed to human nature, and without doubt all human beings were born with the same nature.

He laid the greatest of emphasis on earning money lawfully. But hoarding even lawfully earned wealth was not approved of by him. He advised his followers to place their trust in God instead of keeping food and money for the next day. He also enjoined upon his disciples never to do wrong in return for the wrong done to them. And he insisted that, instead of hitting back, they should pray to God for the guidance of their opponents.

He did not want his disciples to be involved in the world, for he thought that most of their time should be spent in the worship of God and service of His creatures. To attain a high status in the eyes of God, they had to try to fast regularly during the day and spend the night in prayer.

Another very important piece of advice which he gave to his followers was to speak only when necessary, and otherwise remain silent. The reason being that speech is a great gift of God, and one should use it only to earn God's approval. Misusing it would inevitably incur His displeasure.

Khwaja Muinuddin also believed, like Rabia Basri, in the concept of an ecstatic love for God. He held that one who loved God in the true sense, would not fail to love His creatures. He used to say that the most exalted kind of worship was to help the poor and the needy and to feed the hungry. Those who loved both the Creator and the creature were friends of God.

According to *Sururus Sudur* (pp. 46-7), Khwaja Muinuddin believed that assisting the helpless and feeding the hungry were the most superior forms of worship: "All those possessing the following three virtues are friends of God: munificence like an ocean, kindness like the sunshine and humility like the earth."

After settling in Ajmer, the Khwaja married the daughter of a brother of the local governor. His second wife was the daughter of a local Hindu chieftain.

The Khwaja's simple and ascetic life was an inspiration to both Hindus and Muslims. They found in him a sincere spiritual guide. In those days Hindu society was shackled by a rigid caste system. Humanity was categorized according to lower and higher birth. Justice was not done to the lower classes as they were regarded as inferior by birth. When these people saw that the Khwaja treated all human beings alike, without the slightest discrimination, nothing could stop them from coming closer to him. He looked after these poor and needy people like his own brothers and sisters. Not only did he fulfill their physical needs, but he also took full care of their spiritual needs. However, the Khwaja never attempted to convert them to Islam. It was the Islamic concept of the equality of all human beings that played a great role in bringing them into the fold of Islam. They themselves found a religion which treated everyone on an equal footing irresistible. Even to this day, both Hindus and Muslims throng his shrine in Ajmer. He was popularly known as Khwaja Gharib Nawaz.

Thus the stay of Khwaja Muinuddin in Ajmer brought about a far-reaching spiritual and social revolution, (K.A. Nizami) and his teachings still form the most important part of the Chishti life. He died in Ajmer at the ripe old age of 97 and was buried there at Ajmer where he had spent most of his life. Khwaja Husain Nagauri built a tomb over his grave.

Khwaja Muinuddin had two highly able and talented disciples—Shaykh Hamiduddin of Nagaur and Shaykh Qutbuddin Bakhtiar Kaki. Shaykh Hamduddin's real name was Muhammad. His father, Ahmad, had migrated from Lahore to Delhi, where Muhammad was born in 1192. His father attached great importance to education. Therefore Muhammad was properly educated in Arabic, Persian, and religious sciences.

Shaykh Hamiduddin was of a highly spiritual disposition, and lived a very simple and austere life. Although the Chishti saints were allowed to receive cash gifts, he preferred to work for his living. He had a small plot of land in a village called Suwali near Nagaur. He made his living solely from the income from this land. He did not accept any offerings.

He was so sensitive that he did not allow any harm to be done to any form of life. That is why he asked his followers to have only vegetarian food. This also shows his sensitivity to those of his fellow men who were vegetarians.

These Sufis were, in fact, humanitarians par excellence. They did not love Muslims alone, but rather loved all human beings for the simple reason that they were God's creatures. And one who loves God in the true sense can never despise His creatures. These noble human values, cherished by the Sufis, were in fact so contagious that Islam spread among the masses like wildfire.

Shaikh Hamiduddin, being a religious scholar, had a good grasp of Islamic sciences. In fact, he believed that ignorance was the greatest curse for man. He once likened human beings without knowledge to fossils. (*Sururus Sudur,* p. 124)

He believed that the Shariah and Tariqa were interrelated, just as the body and soul are. Treading the path of God and the Prophet to him meant of severing all relations from everything which was not God, and persevering in the pursuit of God alone. That is to say that man should pass each and every moment immersed in thoughts of God, and all his words and deeds should conform to the will of God. If one was involved in the world, he would not be able to concentrate on thoughts of God. Now the question arose of human beings having a physical existence and needing worldly things for their sustenance. They could not cut themselves off from ordinary existence and still survive. On this score, the Sufis maintained that they were allowed to take from the world only what was necessary for their survival. Hamiduddin was particularly very strict about hoarding anything even for the next day. He felt that this mentality of greed could never be satisfied. However much we might hoard. we would always be looking for more and more. Therefore, we should opt for the precious value of contentment in the matter of worldly riches, and set our sights on spiritual gain, for that alone could give us true fulfillment. This would be beneficial not only in this world but also in the world hereafter.

Shayh Hamiduddin shunned fame. He once observed: "The Sufis who sought fame in their own lifetime were soon forgotten, while those who refrained from worldly fame and honour achieved long-lasting fame on their death." (*Fuwaidul Fwad,* pp. 4-5).

Accumulating wealth was anathema to him. He hated hoarding. He likened saved up wealth to a deadly snake. *Sururus Sudur* records a conversation between him and Shaikh Bahauddin, who did not take hoarding so seriously. Hamiduddin said to him: "Wealth is a serpent and one who stores wealth in fact rears a serpent."

Shaykh Bahauddin, who was very rich, was not convinced by this argument. Finally, Shaykh Hamiduddin concluded his arguments by saying that the Suharwardis' achievements as dervishes were not greater than those of the Prophet Muhammad, who had often remarked that his poverty was his pride. The conclusiveness of this argument left Shaykh Bahauddin speechless.

He considered self-effacement a prerequisite if communion with God was to be established. True peace could be attained only by divine grace and, to secure divine grace, the renunciation of all worldly concerns was a sine qua non.

Shaykh Hamiduddin died in November 1274 and lies buried in Nagaur. Sultan Muhamamd bin Tughlaq built a tomb over his grave.

A number of Shaykh Hamiduddin's descendants continued his mission and Nagaur gradually developed into a strong centre of Sufism. This to a great extent was due to Khwaja Husain Nagaur, a descendant of Shaykh Hamid Khwaja Husain who, following in the footsteps of Shaykh Hamiduddin, lived a very simple life . Although he was a religious scholar, he cultivated his land himself. He wrote a commentary on the Quran entitled *Nurun Nabi*, and compiled a number of treatises on Sufism. He also wrote a biography of Imam Ghazali. He attached great importance to education, and devoted himself to the religious and spiritual education of the people.

Khwaja Zia Nakhshabi was the best known disciple of Shaykh Farid, the grandson of Hamiduddin. He was a scholar and a Sufi poet. His book, titled *Silkes Suluk* (String of Sufism) deals with the basic principles of the Sufi mission in 151 short chapters. He regarded a good knowledge of the shariah as being necessary to the understanding of Sufism.

In one of these treatises, it is very interesting to note that he advises the ulama to follow the Sufis in the path of renunciation and the Sufis to follow the ulama on religious matters. He goes on to say: "Without some of the qualities of a dervish an *alim* is like an animal and a dervish without *ilm* (knowledge) is not worthy of undertaking his spiritual journey."

A well-known work of Nakhshabi's is *Tuti Nama* (Stories from a Parrot). This is based on the Persian version of the Sanskrit work titled *Suka Saptati*. Nakhshabi rearranged it and made many changes in it. His style is lucid and very readable. His writings show that, to him, Islam was a religion which advocated a middle path. He said that the Prophet of Islam wanted us to follow the path of moderation, which was good for us both in this world as well as in the next. Nakhshabi died in 1351.

Khwaja Qutbuddin Bakhliar Kaki

THE CHISHTI ORDER became established in Ajmer and Nagaur, thanks to the efforts of Khwaja Muinuddin Chishti and Hamiduddin Nagauri respectively. They were succeeded by worthy disciples who worked hard to spread the teachings of the order.

By the time Khwaja Qutbuddin came to Delhi, the political scene had changed. Sultan Shamshuddin Iltutmish (1210-35) had moved his capital to Delhi, for now Delhi had become the only abode of peace in the entire region. The Mongols had invaded central Asia and Iran, which meant that the Muslims in those areas had lost their political power to barbarians. People therefore flocked to the capital. These included a large number of scholars and Sufi intellectuals. There were even several princes who chose to leave central Asia in order to come to this safe haven.

It was against this backdrop that Qutbuddin Bakhtiar Kaki arrived in Delhi. He was born at , in the province of Taxartes. When he was just 18 months old, his father died. It then fell to his mother to give him his religious education. Interested in spirituality by birth, he committed the entire Quran to memory and spent most of his time in prayer and meditation.

When he grew up, his mother arranged his marriage. But he took no interest in family life, so he divorced his wife and left for Baghdad. There, in a mosque, he met Khwaja Muinuddin. Greatly impressed by his personality, he became his disciple. After Khwaja Muinuddin left Baghdad, Qutuddin went to Multan, where he met Shaikh Bahauddin Zakariya. After a stay of several years in Multan, he went on to Delhi. Shamsuddin Ilfutmish, who had made Delhi his capital, gave him a warm welcome, and many eminent people came to him for spiritual guidance. But he wanted to stay with his spiritual guide, Khwaja Muinuddin. The Khwaja, however, did not allow him to stay in Ajmer, for he was needed more in Delhi than in Ajmer. Delhi had received an influx of newcomers, including a number of religious scholars, and the message of the order had to be communicated to them.

The immense popularity of Khwaja Qutbuddin among the masses as well as the elite was testified to by the large number of people who visited him daily for guidance. He was, like most of the Sufis, a humanitarian in the real sense of the word, always advising his disciples to help the poor and the needy to the extent that they were able. .When offered the post of Shaikhul Islam by the Sultan, he did not accept it.

The Khwaja regarded *sama* (audition) as a means of inducing a mystical state of ecstasy. He was opposed by the ulama on this account. When the controversy intensified, Kwaja Muinuddin Chishti came to Delhi to discover the cause of the friction. Deeply concerned for his disciple, he finally decided to take Qutbuddin away with him. Members of the public were so pained to see the Khwaja leaving their town that a large number of them followed him with tears in their eyes to bid him farewell. Khwaja Muinuddin was so greatly moved at this sign of affection showered on him by the people that he allowed him to return to them.

Because Khwaja Qutbuddin spent most of his time in devotion, fasting and prayer, he could not find the time to make money, so his family lived in poverty, often having to borrow money from a Muslim grocer for their immediate needs. This they repaid as soon as they could. It seems that most of the time all they could afford was plain bread. That was how the Khwaja came to be known as 'Kaki' (Man of Bread).

The story goes that the death of the Khwaja occurred while he was taking part in a *sama* in the Khanqah of Shaykh Ali Sijzi. At the recital of this verse: "The martyrs of the dagger of *taslim* (surrender) get a new life each moment from the unseen world," (*Fawaidul Fuad* by Amir Hasan Sijzi, pp. 159-60) the Khwaja entered an ecstatic state, from which he did not recover. He died on November 27, 1235, and was buried in Mahrauli.

Khwaja Qutbuddin had a number of disciples, two of whom are well known: Shaykh Badruddin of Ghazna and Shaykh Fariduddin Ganj Shakar of Punjab. Badruddin loved to take part in *sama* and danced in ecstatic states. Unlike other Chishti Sufis, he had political associations. These associations did not, however, prove favourable for the Chishti order to flourish in Delhi. He died in 1258-59 and was buried near the tomb of Khwaja Qutbuddin Bakhtiar Kaki. Now the Chishti order was destined to grow in the propitious atmosphere of Ajodhan, the home of Baba Farid Ganj Shakar.

Shaykh Fariduddin's ancestors came to Punjab from Kabul in the 12th century. Fariduddin was born in 1173 or 1175. His father was a religious scholar and his mother was a God-fearing woman, who spent most of her time in devotions. She lived the life of an ascetic and gave the same spiritual training to her son. Under the influence of his mother, he did not take any interest in worldly activities. Most of his time was devoted to meditation. People took him to be an abnormal child.

When he was eighteen years old he went to Multan to receive further education at a seminary in the mosque of Maulana Minhajuddidn Tirmizi. It was here that he met Khwaja Qutbuddin Bakhtiar Kaki. He was so impressed by his spirituality that he became his disciple. After completing his education he left for Delhi, where he stayed in the Khwajah's *jamaat khana*.

Here too he spent much time in ascetic exercises. When Khwaja Muinuddin came to Delhi, he was greatly impressed by him and prophesied the spiritual heights he would reach. With his Shaykh's permission he also performed a *chilla*, that is, he spent a period of forty days in continuous fasting and spiritual exercises.

His fame spread very fast, and people began flocking to him. With all the attention he was given, he found it difficult to dedicate all his time to his devotions, so he left for Hansi in the district of Hisar. He was not in Delhi when Khwajah Qutbuddin Bakhtiar Kaki died. On hearing the news of his death, he reached Delhi in five days time. The Khwajah had willed Baba Farid to be his successor. Accordingly, Qazi Hamiduddin Nagauri gave Baba Farid the relics the Khwajah had left for him. These were his *khirqa* (gown), turban, stick and wooden sandals. Now Baba Farid settled at Ajodhan, where he remained until his death in 1265.

He lived a very simple and austere life, in a small house built of mud. He felt that a house of bricks was not simple enough for an ascetic to live in. His meagre possessions consisted of a small rug and a blanket. He fasted often, breaking his fast with sherbet, wild fruits and millet bread.

In his house there was a separate cell for meditation. There was no furniture. He slept on the floor and his visitors did likewise.. The shrine, or *jamaat khana*, was run by his disciples, many of whom came from far-off places.. The offerings received were either used by those of his disciples staying in the *jamaat khana* or were distributed among the poor and the needy. Nothing was kept for the following day. Doing so would have amounted to showing a lack of trust in God. God had taken the responsibility for providing for the needs of everyone born on this earth. So instead of spending one's time in hoarding and investing, one had better leave this task to God and spend all one's time in worshipping Him..

The *jamaat khana*, which was managed by Badruddin Ishaaq, was situated at a central place, and a large number of visitors came there daily. They were people from all sections of society, from scholars and merchants to Sufis and Qalandars. Some came there to stay, while others came to seek Baba's blessings. Many people came for *tawiz* (amulets) to ward off different diseases.

One special quality of the life of the *jamaat khana* was that there people were free to discuss different issues.

Nizamuddin Awliya's *Malfuzat* (Conversations) mentions these discussions, which on occasion were held between Muslims and non-Muslims.

With the large number of people visiting him daily — thanks to his popularity — Shaykh Fariduddin found little time for prayers and meditation. He ultimately decided, therefore, to leave his house.

Shaykh Farid was not involved in politics. He kept himself apart from those in power. In most cases, he was held in high esteem by them, except for one Sher Khan, the governor of Multan. On seeing that the governor was unhappy with him, the merchants and the wealthy people stopped sending gifts to the *jamaat kKhana*. This caused the people staying there great hardship.

Whenever anyone wanted spiritual help, Baba Farid found himself always ready to give it, irrespective of whether the seeker of help was a commoner or a member of the nobility. He was so concerned about the spiritual well-being of the people that he even tolerated rude behaviour on their part. He never discriminated between individuals, whether Muslims or non-Muslims. For him, all were human beings and all deserved equal attention. A very interesting story is recorded in *Fuwaiding Fuwad* about how a knife was once presented to Baba Farid. He returned it, saying that he would have preferred a needle instead. A knife was used for cutting, while needles stitched things together. He said that he was there not to cut up hearts but to stitch them together.

This attitude on the part of the Sufis went a long way towards healing the tensions between Hindus and Muslims on the subcontinent. Muslims, who had been regarded as invaders, now came to be regarded as spiritual healers in the garb of Sufis. People flocked to them from far and near to receive their blessings. Their doors were open to all, at any time of the day or night. The lower classes, in particular, who had been neglected for centuries, came strongly under their influence. In effect, the hearts of the people were touched by the Sufi teachings, based as they were on moral and spiritual values. A great number even converted to the faith.

The inculcating of such values as humanity, modesty, patience and fortitude and the cleansing of the heart was the mainstay of this spiritual movement.

Chishti Order-2

THE AIM OF Sufism, to Baba Farid, was to prepare the individual to lead a pious life within society. Its core values were: humility, modesty, patience, fortitude and the purification of the heart.

Baba Farid, being a scholar, composed poems in Arabic, Persian and the local dialect known as Hirdawi. He was very humble. He held the *ulama* in high regard but felt that they were not humble enough, in the way that the Sufis were, to give proper guidance to the people. They neither mixed with them, nor encouraged them to ask questions and seek clarifications. Shaykh Farid did not approve of this self-satisfied indifference on the part of the *Ulamas* towards the common man. The Sufis were basically humanitarians, but differed from secular humanitarians in the sense that where a secular humanitarian would be concerned with the welfare of the people in this world alone, they were deeply concerned with the good of the people both in this world as well as the next.

The difference between *Shariah*, *Tariqa* and *Haqiqa* was illustrated by Shaykh Farid in these words: the *zakat* of *Shariah* was five dirhams out of 200, the *zakat* of *Tariqa* involved the payment of 195 dirhams out of 200 and the *zakat* of *Haqiqa* was the payment of everything, retaining nothing for oneself. (*Fuwaidul Fuwad,* p. 117).

Shaykh Farid took great pains in the training of his chief disciples, for it was they who would shoulder the responsibility for communicating the message to the people. He held the Sufi responsible for the worldly and spiritual welfare of his disciples. This demanded a close relationship between the teacher and the taught, because only then could the latter have a proper understanding of moral values. He did not even approve of too many formalities in the initiation of a disciple. To him, true initiation had to be performed by holding the hands of the disciple and praying for his spiritual well-being.

Shaykh Farid had a large family. He had two wives and was survived by five sons and three daughters, some of his children having died in infancy. His eldest son, Nasiruddin, who was an agriculturalist, was a very spiritual person. He spent most of his time in prayer and meditation. Shaykh Nasiruddin's son, Shaykh Kamaluddin, settled in Dhar in Malwa. There, he earned great renown as a Sufi and was popular both with the masses and the nobility. Sultan Mahmud Khalij of Malwa, one of his admirers, had a tomb erected over his grave.

His second son, Shihabuddin worked with Nizamuddin Awliya. The third son, Badruddin Sulaiman also adopted the same Chishti path. His family produced several Sufis of renown, thanks to whose hard work the Chishti order spread throughout India. Badruddin's son, Shaikh Alauddin, was a great Sufi of his times, who spent his whole life in spiritual exercises aimed at self-mortification. He was held in high esteem by Sultan Muhammad bin Tughlaq who built a tomb for him after his death near the burial place of his grandfather.

Of Shaykh Farid's three daughters, one, Bibi Sharifa was widowed at an early age and did not remarry. She spent most of her time in prayer and *zikr*. Shaikh Farid often said that if women could be Khalifas, she would definitely qualify for this honour.

Baba Farid had seven very distinguished Khalifas, Shaikh Nizamuddin Awliya being the most prominent.

The Khalifas of Baba Farid

SHAYKH NAJIBUDDIN MUTAWWAKIL, the younger brother of Baba Farid, lived the life of an ascetic in Delhi and had many disciples. From time to time he visited Ajodhan to receive the blessings of Baba Farid. He died in Delhi and his grave is located close to that of Khwaja Qutbuddin. Sultan Mohammad bin Tughlaq built a tomb at his grave.

Mawlana Badruddin Ishaq, another Khalifa of Shaykh Farid, and also the Shaykh's son-in-law, managed the affairs of the *jamaat khana*, where he used to teach the Quran. He was a Delhiite and had received a proper religious education. He was such a pious person that his eyes were often filled with tears. He died soon after his mentor's death.

Shaykh Jamaluddin of Hansi was both a scholar and a poet. Before he became the Khwaja's disciple, he had been a rich man, but he later renounced all material comforts for the sake of spiritual gain. The Khwaja trusted him in all matters, even authorizing him to endorse the *Khilafat Nama* issued to the disciples by the Khwaja. Two of his books, *Mulhimat*, a collection of Sufi aphorisms written in Arabic, and his *Diwan*, written in Persian, have survived.

Shaykh Arif was another Khalifa, but finding himself unable to perform the requisite duties, he came to Baba Farid and asked to be excused. Baba Farid then asked him to go on a pilgrimage.

Another Khalifah was the famous Sufi, Shaykh Alauddin Ali Sabir, the founder of the Sabiri branch of the Chishti order. His tomb is in Kaliyar, near Roorkee in U.P.

Shaykh Nizamuddin Awliya

SHAYKH NIZAMUDDIN AWLIYA, the celebrated Khalifa of Baba Farid, was the most popular mystic personality of the fourteenth century in India. His grandfather had migrated from Bukhara to Badayun in the state of Uttar Pradesh, and Nizamuddin was born there in 1238. His father died when he was hardly five years old. His mother, being a very pious lady, spared no effort to give her son the best education available in Badayun. First he learned and memorized the Quran. Then he studied books of *fiqh*, *hidaya* and q*uduri* under Abul Hasan Ahmad. He was subsequently allowed to go to Delhi for further studies at the age of 16. There he happened, with great good fortune, to find a place to stay in the neighbourhood of Shaykh Najibuddin Mutawakkil. Then he used to hear from Shaykh Najib about Baba Farid of Ajodhan. By this time Nizamuddin had mastered the Hadith and *fiqh*, on the strength of which accomplishments he felt he might secure the position of Qazi, for his family, now reaching the point of near starvation, was in dire need of resources. He therefore requested Shaykh Najib to pray for his appointment as such, but the Shaykh discouraged him from aspiring to such a post.

Under the influence of Shaykh Najib and often hearing from him about Baba Farid, Nizamuddin finally decided to commit himself to leading the life of a dervish. He left Delhi for Ajodhan in 1257 to meet Shaykh Fariduddin. Baba Farid, quick to gauge his spiritual potential, gave him a warm welcome, and initiated him into the order. Nizamuddin showed great interest in learning ascetic exercises. He spent most of his time in fasting, prayer and meditation, for Baba Farid told him: "Fasting is the first half of the path the Sufi has chosen for himself, and prayers and pilgrimages the other. "

What is notable is that Baba Farid did not discourage him from giving up his studies in favour of supererogatory prayers, for he believed that the one complemented the other. Genuine Sufis have generally attached great importance to religious education. Once Nizamuddin Awliya said: "An illiterate Shaykh is overcome by Satan. A good background of religious education serves as strong defence to ward off the temptations of Satan."

During his second visit Baba Farid taught him some chapters of the Quran, highlighting the spiritual aspects of the verses. Besides this, he also taught him *Awariful Maarif* and *Tamhid* of Abu Shakur. Now Nizamuddin had received full training. On his third visit, in 1265, he was given the *khilafat nama* by Baba Farid. This put it on record that he had completed his spiritual course under Baba Farid and had permission to disseminate his teachings. The Baba also advised him to lead an ascetic life and gave him his blessings in these beautiful words:

"You will be a tree under whose shadow the people will find rest. You should strengthen your spirits by devotion to God."

After his return from Ajodhan, he stayed in Delhi for some time. But he had no place of his own in which he could make a permanent home. He did not earn any money, as all his time was spent in the study of the Quran, prayer and meditation. He lived therefore in deprived circumstances. Finally, he moved to Ghayaspur, a small village near Kilu Khari. It was an unknown place, with no habitation or resources of any kind.

Sultan Muizzuddin Kaiqubad (1287-90) made Kilu Khari his capital. It was only two kilometres away from Ghayspur, which eventually became a busy suburb of Delhi. Now Nizamuddin wanted to move from there, but a Sufi discouraged him from doing so by pointing out that, wherever he went, people would flock to him. He asked him if he would spend his whole life moving from one place to another, and stressed that it was his duty to spread God's message when He had given him the ability and every opportunity to do so. In his case, fleeing from the public would amount to shirking his duty and would incur God's displeasure. Ultimately, Nizamuddin abandoned the idea. Under Sultan Alauddin Khalji (1296-1315) this locality became quite prosperous and densely populated. A number of people, both rich and poor, the common man and the elite, the soldiers and the powerful started visiting him there.

Shaykh Nizamuddin's continuous efforts showed the desired result. People's lives were changing. So many individuals who had just been Muslims in name alone were given the opportunity to understand the true spirit of Islam. Non-Muslims also came to him in great numbers to imbibe moral and spiritual values. The majority of them finally entered his fold, impressed as they were by his personality, his genuineness, and particularly the spiritual interpretation he put upon the teachings of Islam.

Shaykh Nizamuddin took no interest in building good relations with the kings and nobility. Some sultans and noblemen had great regard for the Shaykh while others, such as Sultan Mubarak Shah and Ghyasuddin Tughlaq, took such disinterestedness on the part of the Shaykh as a form of arrogance. They wanted to harm him but, by God's grace, they were unable to do so.

In actual fact, the popularity of Shaykh Nizamuddin was not taken kindly either by the political or the religious leaders. The *Ulama* (religious scholars) too became envious of his popularity. When they saw that even kings could do him no harm, they made a religious issue of the controversial *sama* (audition) and lodged a complaint against him with the king. The Sultan invited the religious scholars to explain to him whether *sama* was Islamic or un-Islamic. The subject was then discussed in great detail.. One Maulana Alamuddin, a grandson of Shaykh Bahauddin Zakariya, who had even written a book on the subject of *sama*, explained it — probably to the king's satisfaction, for he did not take any action against the Shaykh. Thus this conspiracy against the Shaykh likewise failed to harm him, and he continued to work as before till his last breath in

1325. When he felt that the time had come for him to leave this world, he appointed his khalifas so that the mission would continue after his death.

Muhammad bin Tughlaq had a dome constructed over his grave. Both Hindus and Muslims came in large numbers to his tomb to receive his blessings.

People came to him daily in such large numbers that he acquired a vast experience of dealing with all types of individuals. Being very sensitive, he developed a deep insight into human nature and was able to satisfy most of his visitors. Even the religious scholars, who were very reluctant to acknowledge anyone, found his discourses very inspiring. We find from *Awariful Maarif* how adept he was at imparting spiritual instruction, illustrating his points through interesting anecdotes.

Shaykh Nizamuddin believed that first of all one had to be a good human being and only then could one be a good Muslim or a good Hindu. He would often tell this hadith to his disciples: "Whatever you would not like to be done to yourself, do not wish it to happen to others. Wish for others what you wish for yourself." He was a humanitarian par excellence, attaching the greatest of importance to service to humanity after performing obligatory worship.

In his eyes, renouncing the world was a great virtue. Without this he felt that one could not be a good believer. But renouncing the world, in his view, did not mean going so far as to give up even basic necessities. Renunciation, for him, meant that one's heart should be free from the love of the world, for material greed was anathema to any kind of spiritual attainment. If our minds were mired in material things, they lost their proper focus on spiritual matters. He held that the love of the world would even render our prayers and fasting worthless. Once he defined renunciation, or a state of asceticism, as continuing to wear clothing and eating and drinking, but willingly distributing the surplus to the poor and needy, instead of saving it up for the following day.

He did not discriminate between Hindus and Muslims. They were all God's creatures, equally worthy of respect and deserving of help whenever it was needed. Shaykh Nizamuddin's *langar* (free food) was served to both Hindus and Muslims.

Islam to him was not a set of hollow rites and rituals. It was rather a superior ethical code. At times he felt how unfortunate it was that Muslims, preoccupied as they were with the rituals of religion, failed to delve deeper into the spirit of Islam — and this too despite the number of traditions there were which made it clear that God would not accept prayer or fasting unless performed in the correct spirit.

There was not the slightest trace of the communal in the thinking of Shaykh Nizamuddin. He was the epitome of tolerance, broadmindedness and lack of bias. Once, seeing a group of Hindus at worship, he observed: "Every community has its own path and faith, and its own way of worship." He taught his disciples to keep the peace at all times and to develop good relations with everyone, irrespective of caste, colour or creed. For Islam does not teach violence against or discrimination between human beings. Only *taqwa* (the virtue of being God-fearing) — and certainly not material grandeur

— can raise one's status in the eyes of God. . He thus devoted his entire life to bringing people closer to the true spirit of religion

The Shaykh held that *nafs* (the animal soul) was responsible for all evil and that this baser self could be controlled only by spiritual exercises, worship and meditation. He did not, however. ask his disciples to shirk their responsibilities towards their families. He knew full well that it was not everyone who could become a total ascetic. The only thing he disapproved of was the mentality which saved money in excess of need. For example, clothes were necessary to cover the body, but the greed to have more and more spare clothing just to hoard it was quite un-Islamic. Moreover, charity which was just for show undoubtedly incurred God's displeasure. All our actions were judged by our intentions. Only if good acts were done with the pure intention of pleasing God, would they merit any reward from Him.

Amir Khusro, the famous Persian poet, was the Shaykh's most beloved disciple, who in return loved the Shaykh more than anyone else. A Turk, he was born in Balkh. After the Mongol invasion his father, Amir Saifuddin Mahmud, had migrated to India. Thanks to his exceptional abilities, Amir Khusro served under a number of sultans and governors.

Besides being a prolific writer, he also invented several musical instruments including the sitar, and composed a number of melodies based on a mixture of Persian and Indian themes. These were used in *sama* rituals, in which he also participated. In spite of his having too many engagements at court, he always managed to find time to visit his Shaykh.

When the Shaykh died, he happened to be on an expedition to Bengal with Sultan Ghayasuddin Tughlaq. When he heard of his pir's death, he rushed back to Delhi. He could not bear the shock, and his sorrow was so overwhelming that he could not even weep. He lived on for only another six months. He died in September 1325.

Another disciple, Amir Hasan Sijzi, born in Badayun in 1254, was also, like Amir Khusro, a poet and a courtier. He wrote qasidas, a eulogistic poem, and ghazals. He became Shaykh Nizamuddin's disciple at the age of 52. His greatest contribution to posterity is the record he kept of the conversations of Nizamuddin Awliya, titled *Fuwaidul Fuwad*. At one point, when he confided in his mentor that he did not take as much interest in performing obligatory prayers as he did in listening to *sama,* the Shaykh advised him to devote more time to the recitation of the Quran than to the writing of poetry. Hasan did not marry. He died at Daulatabad in 1336.

Ziauddin Barni, the author of *Tarikh-i-Firoz Shahi,* was one of the eminent ulamas and scholars who accepted Shaykh Nizamuddin as their spiritual guide and regularly visited him. Barni wrote a book on Sufism but it has not survived. Once Barni asked Shaykh Nizamuddin why he was not more discriminating in his acceptance of disciples. The Shaykh replied that it was true that previously the pirs had accepted only those disciples who showed total detachment from all that was not godly. But later, in the times of Shihabuddin Suhrawardi and Baba Farid, people came in large numbers to the Sufis wanting to be accepted as disciples.

They belonged to all classes, from the common man to the elite, and all were enrolled by the Sufis as disciples. These disciples refrained from indulging in sin, and offered prayers, both obligatory and non-obligatory. "If I were to impose difficult conditions on them, they would be deprived of even that level of piety," he remarked. He then added that his mentor, Baba Farid, had commanded him to refuse none who turned to him for guidance.

This was evidently a valid point. For the work of reform, which was largely a matter of internal discipline, could be performed only gradually. If people were expected to become perfect in one single day, that would be just so much wishful thinking. Even the Quran endorsed this unhurried, patient way of doing things. For instance, drinking was banned in three stages. In any case, man, being a thinking animal, could adopt something wholeheartedly only when his mind was satisfied that the path he was about to tread was the true one. Thus the rite of initiation into any order was not the end of the story. It was only a beginning. It was a vow to recondition the mind, and a resolve to sincerely follow the path shown by the mentor.

The Khalifas of Shaykh Nizamuddin

QAZI MUHIUDDIN KASHANI was one of Shaykh Nizamuddin'ss senior Khalifas. After becoming the Shaykh's disciple, he abandoned worldly life in favour of asceticism. The Shaykh accorded him great respect and It is on record that he wrote out the *Khilafat Nama* for him with his own hands. Here is one point which he added to this document:

"Lead the life of an ascetic; pay no attention to the things of this world and its authorities. Do not accept gifts from rulers."

Maulana Wajihuddin Yousuf of Chanderi, Maulana Shamsuddin, son of Yahya, who was settled in Delhi, and Shaykh Qutbuddin Munawwar, who was settled in Hansi, were some of the other important Khalifas.

Maulana Husamuddin of Multan, a scholar, was a notable Khalifa, who stayed for some time in the Kilu Khari Mosque. Living in a thatched hut, he led a very simple life. On one occasion he asked the Shaykh about the acceptance of loans. The Shaykh replied that there could be only two reasons for accepting a loan: one to maintain one's family and the other to provide for the needs of travellers. However, the Shaykh added that loan seeking and repayment disturbed the spiritual routine of a dervish. Therefore, a true ascetic had better stay away from money matters.

On another occasion Shaykh Nizamuddin, addressing Maulana Hesamuddin, gave a six-point formula to facilitate the intense concentration on God by which a Sufi could realize his goal:

1. One should retire to a lonely place, without desiring any company or change.

2. One should always be in a state of cleanliness. One may sleep when necessary but, on rising, one should immediately perform one's ablutions.

3. One should keep an unbroken fast.

4. Either one should perform *zikr* or remain silent.

5. While reciting *zikr*, one should recollect in one's heart the presence of one's pir.

6. Every thought except that of God should be expelled.

After moving his capital to Daulatabad, Sultan Mohd bin Tughlaq transferred the ulama and Sufis, including Maulana Hesamuddin, to Daulatabad. From there he left for *livipiral* where he died.

Maulana Fakhruddin Zarradi is another notable Sufi who was also an *alim*. When he met Shaykh Nizamuddin, he was so impressed by his personality and his intellectual capability that he decided to become his follower. Most of his time was spent in prayer. He rented a home near the *jamaa*t, so that he remained close to his Shaykh. His fame spread far and wide.

Maulana Alauddin Nili, another Khalifa, is known for his transcription of *Fuwaidul Fuwad*.

Maulana Burhamuddin Gharib was yet another Khalifa, who invented a new style of dancing during the ritual of *samas*, known as Burhani. He too was compelled to leave Delhi for Daulatabad. There he became so well-known that Sultan Nasir Khan Faruqi (1399-1437) built a town called Burhanpur in his name.

Another Khalifa of Shaykh Nizamuddin was Shaykh Akhi Sirajuddin Usman, who was born in Lakhnauti. To embark on a course of spiritual education, he came to Delhi and stayed in the *jamaat khana*. After completing his studies, he left Delhi and went back to Lakhnauti. There he gained a great number of converts both from the masses as well as the elite, including the rulers.

Shaykh Nasruddin Mahmud was the most prominent of the Shaykh's Khalifas. He was also his chief successor in Delhi. He is popularly known as the 'Chiragh' (lamp) of Delhi. He was born in Awadh in 1276. His father, a wool merchant, died when he was hardly nine years of age. His mother wanted him to complete his secular education, but he did not take any interest in worldly matters even in his childhood. At the age of 25 he abandoned the world in favour of the life of a Sufi. He spent all his time in fasting, prayers and in exercises of self-mortification. He would feed himself on wild leaves. He used to go off to lonely places, often by some tombs, where he would pray the whole day.

Now, Shaykh Nizamuddin had a number of disciples in Awadh, — Nasruddin's birthplace — his order having spread there. Shaykh Nasruddin, as a result of being in contact with these disciples, decided to migrate to Delhi at the age of 43 in order to become the Shaykh's disciple. By that time he had already performed rigorous spiritual exercises and had fully prepared himself for this path. The Shaykh greeted him cordially and duly initiated him as his disciple.

Chishti Order-3

SHAYKH NASIRUDDIN, HAVING led a long life of prayer and meditation in a solitary place, did not feel at ease in urban surroundings. He wanted therefore to retire to the jungles and mountains. But his pir did not allow him to lead his life in seclusion. He was asked instead to remain in Delhi among the people and suffer whatever hardship it entailed. For the Shaykh, all kinds of experiences were necessary for his intellectual and spiritual development. Besides, those who had been blessed with the realization of God, had a duty to guide the people along that same path. If the realized souls shirked their duty by opting for a life of retirement in the jungles, that would amount to risking divine displeasure.

Shaykh Nasiruddin was regarded as a great source of spiritual bounty, that is why people named him 'Ganj', the treasury.

Taking note of the popularity of the Sufis, Sultan Muhammad Tughlaq tried to pressurize them into helping in his ambitious schemes. Those who refused to do so were made to suffer for it. Shaykh Nasiruddin was also one of those under pressure, but he somehow managed to escape going to Daulatabad.

After the death of Sultan Muhammad bin Tughlaq in 1351, Firoz, a cousin of his, succeeded him with the help of the ulama, the Sufis and certain courtiers. He developed good relations with the religious and spiritual leaders. He used to shower gifts on them, but Shaykh Nasiruddin continued to live the same life of poverty and austerity. When he was visited by Sultan Firoz, he did not accord him any special treatment.

One day while he was engaged in solitary meditation, he was stabbed so grievously by a qalandar named Turab that the blood flowed from his wound. His disciples ran to attack the qalandar, but he restrained them from doing so, saying that he had already forgiven him. The Shaykh survived the wound and his prayers and fasting continued as usual. He died three years after the attack in September 1356.

Shaykh Nasiruddin had a large number of disciples but, either they were not worthy, in his eyes, of inheriting the relics of his pir, Shaykh Nizamuddin, or he did not want to part with them even after his death. So, according to his will, these relics were buried with his body. The Khirqa was placed on his ribs, the staff was laid beside his body, etc. His final message for his disciples was:

"Everyone has to bear the burden of his own faith. There is no question of bearing the burden of others."

A tomb was built for him by Sultan Firoz. It is situated in the area known as Chiragh-i-Dehli.

The teachings of Shaykh Nasiruddin have been preserved in a book written by Hamid Qalandar. By this time, the ethics of the Chishti philosophy had been fully developed.

There were two categories of followers, one, that of the common people who were expected to do some *wadifas* given to them by their Shaykhs, lead a morally upright life and avoid sin as much as possible. Apart from this, they were allowed to engage in worldly activities. In the other category were those who had dedicated themselves fully to the spiritual path. As such, they were not allowed to go to the market place to make money. They were to have full trust in God and pray to God for all their spiritual and material needs, spending all their time in worship and in the activities of the order. Life had been bestowed upon them by God, so they had to devote their lives to the service of God. This became possible only by severing all relationships with everything but God.

It is essential that our attention should not be unnecessarily given to irrelevant and trivial affairs. It is only when all our thoughts are centred on God, that we are properly focused: all other thoughts are then automatically marginalized, for our minds cannot focus on two things at one and the same time. It is only by concentrating on God and God alone that the objective of establishing contact with Him will be achieved as desired. Ultimately, it is the love of God which will drive away all other thoughts.

Shaykh Nasiruddin believed that a Sufi was obliged to lead a very hard life. For a life of comfort was an obstacle to realizing God. He had to keep his eating, sleeping and talking to the barest minimum, and try to stay away from people, because they would not allow him to concentrate on his objective; concentration was a must for any degree of spiritual gain. Time was of the utmost importance and if spent to no good purpose, it was lost and could never be recovered. Therefore, the Sufi's time had to be spent largely in learning the meaning of the Quran and in contemplation (KM p.109). He who prayed and meditated in the solitude of the early morning would be the one to experience the divine light in his soul.

The Chishtis laid the greatest of emphasis on breathing control practiced during meditation. They believed that control of the breath prevented the thought processes from being diverted. This also ensured that the Salik's (disciple) time was fully utilized.

With every inhaling and exhaling of the breath, some phrases from the Quran were recited and God's name was invoked. Once the Sufis were able to control their breathing through practice, they could rest assured that their time would not be wasted. Concentration exercises were given great importance in almost every order. These methods of breath control were and still are in vogue among yogis during meditation.

Shaykh Nasiruddin did not think that being in government service was an obstacle to contemplation and meditation. He also made it clear that Sufism had nothing to do with externals like wearing some special type of clothing or a particular kind of cap. To him, Sufism concerned the training of the mind. It disciplined one's inner self.. When the mind was fully trained to concentrate on God, no engagement could distract the Sufi's attention. Once the mind was properly attuned, nothing could come in the way of God's remembrance. One could be engaged physically in worldly affairs, but mentally one would be in the vicinity of God. However, it was understood that this worldly engagement should be purely for the purpose of securing the necessities of life and not aimed at acquiring comforts and luxuries. For greed had no end. One would never be satisfied with worldly acquisitions — not till one's dying day. Thus the Sufi or spiritual way to make a living was to earn according to one's need, and not according to one's greed.

After Shaykh Nasiruddin the centre of the spiritual empire of the Chishti Sufis had been shifted from Delhi to different places, mainly in the south. The most important of these was the Sabriyyah branch, founded by Ala al-Din Ali ibn Ahmad Sabir (d. 1291) at Kaliyar in U.P., in which state a number of branches were established by his successors. Ahmad Abdul Haq of Rudawli and Shaykh Abdul Quddus Gangohi were distinguished Sufis of this order. Shaykh Muhibbullah Sadrupuri of Allahabad, a successor of Abdul Quddus Gangohi, was a great religious scholar and an advocate of Ibn Arabi's *wahdatul wajud*. During the 14th and 15th centuries the Sufi spirit was most active in Bengal and the Daccan. Shaykh Sirajuddin of Gawr and Nur Qutb-I-Alan were distinguished Sufis of that period. Shaykh Burhamuddin Gharib (d. 1340), a disciple of Shaykh Nizamuddin, established a Chishti centre in Dawlatabad. He was very popular and so greatly respected by the local ruler that the new city built by him was named Burhanpur after him.

Sayyed Muhammad ibn Yusuf al Husayni, popularly known as Khwajah Banda Nawaz or Gisu Daraz (d. 1422), was the most famous Sufi in the Daccan. He was Shaykh Nasiruddin Chiragh's Khalifa. He was very energetic and worked in a number of different places. He had started his activities in Delhi, but at that time the environment was not favourable there, so he moved to Gujarat; from where he went on to the Daccan. During his last days he shifted to Culbarga, where he worked for about ten years. He was a prolific author and a poet. He was eminently successful in establishing a Chishti centre in the region.

The most notable Chishti Sufi of the Nizami branch in the eighteenth century was Shah Kalimullah Jahanabadi (d. 1729). His dynamic spiritual leadership enthused this order with a new spirit. His successors, the most prominent of whom was Shah Nizamuddin, were active till the eighteenth century and managed to maintain the spiritual life of Delhi. Finally, the centre of activity bifurcated and new centres came to be established in the Punjab, Bareilly and Rajasthan. At present, there are a great number of Chishti centres on the Indian subcontinent which are actively engaged in disseminating the teachings of the Chrishti order.

The Jamaat Khana – a Centre of Peace and Spirituality

ONE OF THE most salient features of the Chishti order was that its members mixed freely with the common man. They did not retire to the jungle and mountains, thinking only of their own spiritual gain, but rather, like Gautam Buddha, they decided to convey the truth to as many people as possible. They even provided board and lodging to their disciples in modest dwellings with mud walls and thatched roofs called *jamaat khanas*. These had quiet, separate places for meditation. They gradually became centres of social and spiritual life. The Shaykh and his family also lived in one part of the building and ate along with the disciples. Those who were associated with this spiritual centre did not go out to make money. They lived on *futuh*, that is, voluntary contributions. Baba Farid was very strict about not keeping gifts for the next day. Whatever was left after all basic needs had been met was distributed to the poor and the needy. For the mentality of storing material things demonstrated distrust in God's bounty. To be a true believer in God, one had to have complete trust in God .Only then would one be held deserving of God's blessings.

The Social Principles Governing the Chishti Spiritual Life

"DO AS YOU would be done by" was a principle given the utmost importance in the social regulation of Chishti life in the *jamaat khana*. Chishtis were not opposed to family life, and since family life necessarily demanded some worldly activities, they were allowed to procure worldly things to serve their needs. But any inclination to store these worldly things was opposed. For instance, the Chishti Sufis were not allowed to keep spare garments.

Although Shaykh Nizamuddin did not marry and many prophets like Yahya and Jesus did not marry, Khwaja Muinuddin did marry, albeit at an advanced age, for marrying was also a tradition of the Prophet. Leading a celibate life, of course, was not a sin, for had it been wrong, no prophet would have remained celibate. What was sinful was to transgress the bounds set by God. Those who were not sure of their ability to lead chaste and pious lives were cautioned not to opt for celibacy.

Shaykh Nizamuddin was not against leading a married life. But he felt that one who desired total involvement in divine contemplation had no need to marry. For being engrossed in divine contemplation was a guarantee that he was protected from committing any sin. But if a Sufi failed to attain such a degree of absorption as would leave no room for sexual desire, then he was advised to opt for married life. Shaykh Nizamuddin felt that full concentration was required for complete absorption in God, and that any involvement in worldly matters was an obstacle to the attainment of this higher state of realization of God.

Laymen who could not dedicate their entire time to this spiritual life were allowed to pursue their worldly activities, the only proviso being that they should do so by honest means. They were even allowed to hold government posts, as in the case of such distinguished disciples as Amir Khusro and Amir Hasan. Everything was seen in terms of its outcome. If such occupations were dedicated to serving mankind, they had full permission to engage in them, but if they led to cruelty, greed and other such moral evils, they were debarred from taking them up.

Chishti Rituals

A FAIR KNOWLEDGE of the Shariah was the minimum qualification for the initiation of the disciples into the order. The first rite to be performed was that of *tawba* (repentance). *Tawba* was the first step towards a new spiritual life, for it redeemed one of a past sinful life. Furthermore, if repentance came from a sincere heart, this served as a safeguard against future sins. Thus *tawba* brought about a complete revolution in one's life. Shaykh Nizamuddin once observed that *tawba* was of two kinds — present and future. The *tawba* for the present required man to feel guilty about past sins and to sincerely regret them and the *tawba* for the future required him to be fully determined never to commit those sins again, that is to refrain from further wrongdoing.

God assures us that no matter what our sins have been, if we truly repent and seek His forgiveness, and take steps to put right our wrongs, He will forgive us.

But the true *tawba* was one which was not a mere repetition of words. Rather it involved offering compensation to those who were wronged. For instance, if someone had stolen money from another, not only had he to repay this amount, but he had also to exert himself to placate the person who had been robbed. If someone abused another, it was necessary for the abuser to approach the abused person and offer him his sincere apologies. Thus *tawba* aimed at revolutionizing the whole life of an individual.

Dhikr means to remember God. One must remember God at all times and in all situations. . When a person has reached this stage, it is an indication that he has found God with all His attributes. *Dhikr* is a spiritual method of concentration, by which God's name is recited in a rhythmical way, the aim being to feel the Divine presence in one's inner being. In the process, one of God's 99 names is generally invoked while controlling the respiration.

The Chishtis generally performed *Dhikr-I-Jali,* which was recited aloud. Sometimes different syllables of the *kalima,* and sometimes one of the names of God were recited. They felt that by invoking God's name, they could establish communion with Him. By reciting God's name continuously, the disciple's whole being was absorbed by the thought of God.

The Chishtis developed the technique of *pas-i-anfas* (controlled breathing) which, according to Shaykh Nasruddin, was the essence of the Sufi discipline. This was practiced during meditation. The Sufis maintained that when breathing was controlled, thoughts were not diffused, and time was properly utilized. The development of this technique showed the influence of the yogis who also breathed in a measured way..

Sama, a spiritual exercise, was practiced by the Chishtis. *Sama* literally meant a "hearing" or "audition". *Sama,* in relation to *tasawwuf,* meant the use of music as an aid to contemplation, which in turn was aimed at inducing ecstasy. Thus *sama* came to denote listening to music, singing, chanting and measured recitation for the purpose of inducing religious emotions and ecstasy. The Chistis in particular and the Sufis in general were criticized by the ulama for this practice, but they were not ready to abandon it.

Qadiri Order

THE QADIRI ORDER, named after Shaykh 'Abd al-Qadir Jilani (470/1077-561/1166), figures prominently in Islamic spiritual history. Although from the organizational standpoint, it took almost half a century after the death of the saint for it to come to the fore, its teachings strongly influenced the thinking and conduct of a considerable number of Muslims during his lifetime. On account of his noble virtues and his spiritual attainments, the Shaykh was eventually regarded as having reached the peak of perfection.

Shaykh 'Abd al-Qadir had a highly persuasive way of encouraging people to distance themselves from obsessions with material things, and to turn instead to matters of the spirit. Having awakened the spiritual side of their nature, he dedicated himself to instilling in them a profound reverence for moral and spiritual values. His religiosity and earnestness made a great impression on his fellow men, who flocked to his side. He asked that his followers should maintain the same strict standard of adherence to all the ramifications of Islamic Law (*Shariah*) as he did himself, for he looked upon the *Shariah* as the mainspring of all spiritual progress. Insistence upon this point not only forged a bond between the jurists (*faqihs*) and the mystics (Sufis), but also ensured that there would be a just equilibrium between the varying interpretations of the spirit and letter of Islamic Law.

In his works and sermons, he makes frequent mention of Imam Ahmad ibn Hambal (d. 241/855), and in many matters of religious importance, his stance was certainly influenced by his connection with the Hambali School of Islamic jurisprudence

In fact, he made *fiqh* (jurisprudence) and *tasawwuf* (mysticism) complementary to each other and brought jurists and mystics together in their dealings with both subjects .In his elaborations on on mysticism, he was always careful to keep all legal facets in view and, conversely, in explaining the principles of the law, he emphasized their spiritual implications.

Like most Islamic reformers of the Middle Ages, Shaykh 'Abd al-Qadir believed that his mission was inspired by God and that it was at His Will that he led people along the path of spirituality. This awareness gave not only profundity to his mission but also reinforced his endeavours with a sense of divine inspiration. He looked upon himself as God's envoy for the ethical and spiritual revitalization of society. The Shaykh regarded "showing people the way to God" not only as the lynchpin of all mystic striving but as an inheritance of the Prophetic mission, which it was the duty of all Muslims to perpetuate regardless of circumstances. He addressed the problem of inculcating spirituality as a matter of both knowledge and faith. This is evident from the sermons contained in *al-Fath al-rabbani* ("Divine Victory"), which he preached in both *madrasah* (college) and *ribat* (hospice).

The Reform of Islamic Society

'ABD AL-QADIR'S MYSTIC strivings were designed to meet the challenges of the era in which he lived: the decline in both Muslim political power and Muslim morals vitiated social structures, while spiritual life was eclipsed by material obsessions. Shaykh 'Abd al-Qadir's movement for spiritual uplift was so effective that a number of Sufis adopted Qadiri mystic ideals and began to disseminate them. This led to a *silsilah* (chain of a spiritual order) coming into existence, whose aim was a large-scale regeneration of the spiritual culture of society. To begin with, the Qadiri teachings took hold in and around Baghdad, but subsequently their influence was felt also in Arabia, Morocco, Egypt, Turkestan, and India, and people entered the fold in large numbers. The social environment and religious background of these regions being quite diverse in nature, the order had to solve a number of problems relating to local conventions.

Because the Qadiri Order did not take its final shape during the Shaykh's lifetime, many of the spiritual exercises and litanies that were later standardized did not originate in the Shaykh's own teachings. But it was these spiritual exercises which gained the interest of the people. The Shaykh's books, being in Arabic, had a limited impact on people of non-Arab regions. Persian commentaries and translations of his works certainly appeared in India and other countries, but the spiritual standards set by the Shaykh and the doctrines preached by him were so lofty that they could not be followed in scrupulous detail by ordinary men and women. As a result, subsequent generations set greater store by the litanies of the Qadiri Order than the actual teachings of the Shaykh.

The Organization and Dissemination of the Order

IT IS AGAINST the background of the conquest of Baghdad by Hulagu in 658/1258, the fall of Granada in 897/1492, and the rise of the Ottoman Empire in 923/1517 — the three major developments in the Islamic world — that the history of the Qadiri Order evolved in Africa, Central Asia, and Turkestan. Hulagu's sack of Baghdad (658/1258) put an end to the functioning and influence of both the *madrasah* and the *ribat,* and the Shaykh's descendants moved away to many different areas. Those who had close connections with his family then set themselves to organizing the order in different regions. Such family members as stayed behind in Baghdad formed the "moral centre" of the order. Others settled in Cairo and Aleppo.

The Shaykh was both mystic guide and college teacher, but after him these two areas of operation were dealt with separately by one son, 'Abd al-Wahhab (552-1151-593/1196), who took over from him in the *madrasah*, and another son, 'Abd al-Razzaq (528/1134-603/1206-7), who worked in the *ribat*. His mysticism and discipline were propagated in Yemen by 'Ali ibn Haddad. In Syria, Muhammad al-Bata'ini of Baalbek disseminated his religious doctrine with great success. In Egypt, Muhammad 'Abd al-Samad worked for the spread of the order. Indeed, there was a time when the entire Nile Valley was home to a large network of Qadiri centres, and Cairo became an important hub of the Qadiri Order.

The order was introduced into Asia Minor and Istanbul by Ismail Rumi (d. 1041/1631). He founded some forty *takiyyahs* ('Sufi centres' in Turkish) in that region and a *khanqah* ('Sufi centre' in Persian) known as *Qadiri-khanqah*. In Arabia *zawiyahs* ('Sufi centre' in Arabic) were set up at Jedda, Madina, and Mecca. In Africa, there were numerous Qadiri *zawyiahs* at Khartoum, Sokoto, and Tripoli. Qadiri missionary activity was greatly in evidence among the Berbers.

The Life of the Founder

SHAYKH 'ABD AL-QADIR was born in 470/1077-78 in the village of Nif *(Bahjat al-asrar)*, in the district of Gilan in northern Iran (south of the Caspian Sea). He was descended from Imam Hasan, the Prophet's grandson. Orphaned early, he was looked after by his maternal grandfather, Sayyid 'Abd Allah Suma'i, who was a pious and saintly person. When he reached the age of eighteen (in 488/1095), 'Abd al-Qadir left Gilan for Baghdad, which was then the hub of unparalleled intellectual activity and where the reputed Nizamiyyah College, a seminary founded in 457/1065, was at its zenith. However, he chose not to study in this institution and sought the completion of his studies with other teachers of Baghdad.

Right from his early childhood, his truthful character had a great influence on anyone who chanced to meet him. There is a story about his departure from his native place for Baghdad, which illustrates his very special virtues. When he was on the point of leaving, he was given forty gold coins by his mother

—his share in the patrimony. These she concealed by stitching them into his cloak. As parting advice to her son, she told him always to be truthful and honest. 'Abd al-Qadir then promised her that he would never tell a lie.

On the way his caravan was held up by bandits, one of whom asked 'Abd al-Qadir if he was carrying anything of any value with him. He replied that he had forty gold coins. The robber did not believe him and moved on to another victim. One after the other the bandits came and questioned him and he gave them all the same answer. But then the bandit leader asked him to show him where he had kept his money. 'Abd al-Qadir then produced his cloak and the money was found to be concealed in its lining. Startled and puzzled at such truthfulness, the bandit asked him why he had owned up to having something of value; he could have easily said that he had nothing and thus have saved his money. 'Abd al-Qadir replied that he had made a promise to his mother always to be truthful, regardless of the circumstances. This avowal gave a severe jolt to the bandit leader. He thereupon fell at his feet and repented of his wrongdoing, saying: "You keep the promise you made to your mother, while we forget the promise that we made to our Creator." The miscreants returned all of their ill-gotten gains to their victims and repented of their misdeeds.

It was in Baghdad that 'Abd al-Qadir felt drawn to the Hambalite school of Islamic law. This was during the early years when he was in great difficulties because of his lack of means. But poverty and hunger did nothing to dilute his keenness for the acquisition of knowledge. He made a careful study of *Hadith* (sayings of the Prophet), *fiqh* (law), and literature and received his spiritual training from Shaykh Abu'l Khayr Hammad ibn Muslim al-Dabbas (d. 525/1131), an unlettered saint who was famous for his spiritual perfection. At that time Abd al-Qadir was reputed as a jurist, and as such it was not taken well amongst the Sufis that he should become one of them. But since mysticism was looked upon favourably by some of the Hambalite jurists of this period, this antagonism soon dissipated. It is reported that Abd al-Qadir was initiated into the mystic discipline by Qadi Abu Said Mubarak al-Mukharrimi, head of a school of Hambalite law in Baghdad, who bestowed upon him his mystic robe.

Once the Shaykh's academic and spiritual training in Baghdad was over, he withdrew from human affairs, spending eleven years in the ruins near Baghdad in total seclusion. In the words of Henri Bergson this seclusion of a mystic is "like the repose of a locomotive standing in a station under steam pressure." When he re-emerged from his retreat, he began with great energy and keenness to address the public. He did so on the advice — which reinforced his own spiritual leanings — of Khwajah Yusuf Hamadani (d. 534/1140). He figures in the works of all of his contemporaries and later writers as playing an extremely powerful role as a preacher. Many mystics made an impact upon the people by giving them their undivided attention and personal care, but the Shaykh took a different course, addressing vast crowds and bringing about a revolution in their lives.

In Islamic history, his feats were unparalleled. With this resort to mass appeal, Islamic mysticism entered a new stage, when the mystic teachers of *da'irahs* (small mystic centres of like-minded persons) and *zawiyahs* (centres for mystics to live and pray) emerged from their retreats and began to address huge gatherings to whom they communicated their message of spiritual and moral enlightenment. According to Shattanawfi, as many as seventy thousand people came to hear his sermons. *(Bahjat al-asrar,* 92). This may be somewhat in excess of the actual numbers, but there was no doubt about the popularity of his thrice-weekly sermons which were attended by people from Mesopotamia, Persia, and Egypt. Four hundred scribes recorded whatever he uttered (*Bahjat al-asrar,* 95) His meetings were also attended by Jews and Christians, who were so inspired by his eloquence that they often entered the fold of Islam on the spot. Of the impact which he made as a preacher, Abu'l-Faraj al-Jawzi, a contemporary writer, says that as a result of his urgings, people eschewed their evil ways and began to set their feet upon the straight and narrow path of the good and the right. What was even more extraordinary was that members of his congregations sometimes breathed their last as a result of the overwhelming emotions which they experienced as they listened to his words.

Entrusted by his teacher, Qadi Abu Sa'id Mubarak al-Mukharrimi, with the running of a large *madrasah*, the Shaykh paid such attention to its constant improvement that its environs came almost to have the status of a *madrasah* town. The Shaykh himself used to teach several religious sciences. With both the *madrasah* and the *ribat*, the Shaykh had everything he needed at his disposal for the spread of his brand of religion. Over a period of forty years (521/1127-561/1165) he delivered his sermons and gave instruction in religious sciences and, for thirty-five years as *mufti*, he gave his religious opinion (Bahjat al-Asrar, 95). He thus blended with his profound knowledge of Islamic law his mystical fervour for the spiritual life. Though apparently committed ideologically to the Hanbalite school, he evinced a certain broadness of approach for, according to a report, he acted as the guardian of Imam Abu Hanifah's tomb.

During his lifetime, there were certain misgivings about his status as a Sufi teacher. But this was due to a wrong construction having been put on his endeavours. The Shaykh looked after a community centre dedicated to mystic discipline and he himself was totally mystical in his approach. But since the silsilahs were regularly organized only at a later period, his mystic striving was never formalized as a well-constructed methodology. For an ultimately deep and perspicacious presentation of Sufi idealism, one must consult his *Ghunyat al-Talibin* (*That Which Is Sufficient for Seekers*).

'Abd al-Qadir as the Apex

ONE OF HIS greatest achievements was the thorough revitalization of Muslim spiritual culture. Some of the founders of mystic orders—like Khwajah Mu'inuddin Chishti and Shaykh Najibuddin 'Abdul Qahir Suhrawardi— deriving great benefit from directly associating with him, came under the influence of his mystic ideas.

The Works of 'Abd al-Qadir

TWENTY-FOUR TITLES OF manuscripts ascribed to Shaykh 'Abd al-Qadir have been listed by Brockelmann. A study of his treatises is essential if the interpretations of his teachings by succeeding generations are to be put in the correct perspective.

Shaykh 'Abd al-Qadir's mystic and religious ideas are presented in the following works: (1) al-Ghunyah li-talibi tariq al-haqq (*That Which Is Sufficient to the Seekers of the Path of Truth*) (generally known as Ghunyat al-talibin), an exhaustive work on the obligations enjoined by Islam and the Islamic way of life; (2) *al-Fath al-rabbani,* a record of sixty-two sermons delivered by him during the years 545/1150-546/1152; and (3) *Futuh al-ghayb* (Victories of the Invisible), a record of seventy-eight sermons compiled by his son, 'Abd al-Razzaq.

He wrote the *Ghunyat al-talibin,* a detailed account of his religious views, at the request of his followers and friends. It was translated into Persian by 'Abd al-Hakim Sialkoti (d. 1068/ 1657). Unlike the two other works, the *Futuh al-ghayb* and *al-Fath al-rabbani,* this is a comprehensive work on both Islamic Law and mystical thought. His sermons, however, are less than exhaustive, because his compilers were unable to record his every utterance. There were bound to be omissions. In the two collections of his sermons, the Shaykh emerges as being of an entirely otherworldly nature, but in the *Ghunyat* there is a greater equilibrium between spiritual and worldly obligations. His deliberations on faith, charity (*zakat),* fasts, and hajj (pilgrimage) are followed by an analysis of the propriety of behaviour to be observed in daily life and, in one part of this work, he deals with those sects that he considered to have strayed from the true path.. It was in the context of faith, devotion to God, and interaction with his fellow men that the

Shaykh set forth his ideas on religion and ethics. His book ends with an exposition of his mysticism.

The sermons contained in *Futuh al-ghayb* are loosely arranged according to their subject matter but are undated. On the insistence of Shaykh 'Abd alWahhab Qadiri Shadhili of Mecca and Shah Abu'l-Ma'ali of Lahore Shaykh, 'Abd ul-Haqq Muhaddith of Delhi translated *Futuh al-ghayb* into Persian so that the Shaykh's views might be the better disseminated.. The *Fath al-rabbani* gives the substance of the forty sermons the Shaykh delivered either in the *khanqah* or in the *ribat* in 545/1150. It represents a single year of the Shaykh's assemblies, but in this account there are necessarily omissions, mainly because of the scribe's inability to reproduce word for word the sermons of the Shaykh. It has been left to the translators and commentators of his works to fill in the lacunae. Many abridgements, critical revisals and commentaries of his works have also appeared.

It was more than a hundred years after the saint's death that his biography, *BahJat al-asrar (Splendor of Secrets)*, was compiled by 'Ali ibn Yusuf al-Shattanawfi (d. 713/1314)

The Teachings of the Shaykh on Mysticism and Metaphysics

SHAYKH 'ABD AL-QADIR'S spirituality stemmed from his realization of God. For him God was an all-encompassing persona forever immanent in man's moral, intellectual, and aesthetic awareness; He was neither a deified legendary figure nor was He an abstract, rationalized concept of oneness. He felt as if he were always in His Presence. From his sermons it was possible to judge the degree of his own realization of God's Omnipresence This consciousness of the Divine Omnipresence guided and motivated his active waking life and raised it to a transcendental level. The Prophet's urging of people "to pray as if you see Him; and if you see Him not then He sees you" was his most important maxim and he certainly practiced what he preached. He believed that this realization made each individual's heart pure and thus attuned it to the realm of the Spirit *(al-Fath al-rabbani,* XXIII 1'33) without, however, losing sight of the separateness of the Creator and His creation. On the other hand, his analyses of *fana'* (annihilation) and *baqa'* (subsistence) erred on the side of caution, in that they carefully skirted the subject of pantheism, although many later Qadiri saints, such as Miyan Mir (d. 1045/1635) and Mulla Shah Badakhshani (d. *'1071/1661)* of India were not so scrupulous in their approach.

Total devotion to God constituted the ideal life for the Shaykh. He considered that it was for this sole purpose that God created mankind. The Quran says, "I have not created *jinn* and mankind except to serve Me." (LI, 56). A "God-conscious existence" gives man superior spirituality; it raises him above the worldly grind for insignificant advancement; it shows him how hollow are the supposed "joys of life"; it introduces him to spiritual tranquillity and makes it possible for him to have access to the true source of spiritual power. The more a man endeavours to "live for the Lord; the nearer he comes to realizing the divine purpose of life. One has to surrender his life, his will, and his material means to God if he aims at divine realization." *(al Path al-rabbani,* XXI, 122-25).

Man is endowed with spiritual strength, however, only when he is at one with the Divine Purpose of Existence and leads his life in accordance with the Divine Will as revealed in the *Sunnah* (sayings and doings of the Prophet). All those who scrupulously follow the guidance of the *Sunnah* in all aspects of day-to-day living in effect submit themselves to the Divine Will.

The Shaykh considered that the world of the hereafter was veiled from our eyes by this present world. The greater the degree of involvement in this world and all its attractions, the more dense the veil (*hijab*) between man and the unknowable world of the afterlife. *(al-Fath al rabbani,* XXI, 122).

The seeker after further spiritual enlightenment must leave behind the ego and eschew attachments to all worldly, material things. Remaining embroiled in worldly matters de-sensitizes man spiritually and renders him incapable of responding to the word of God. On the question of detachment, the Shaykh went so far as to say that without distancing oneself entirely, both physically and mentally, from the surrounding world, one remains dormant as a spiritual being. Constant endeavour and an intelligent approach are essential for spiritual progress. He held that a truly spiritual existence was impossible unless one kept a tight rein on one's natural inclinations and invariably bowed to the dictates of the *Shari'ah* on all matters, whether in connection with food and drink, wearing apparel, the marriage bond, or even ingrained habits and preferences. In support of his doctrine, he quoted this verse from the Quran: "Whatever the Messenger gives you, take; whatever he forbids you, give over." (LIX, 7) *(Futuh al-ghayb, 159)*

The Origins of Human Thinking

FOR THE GUIDANCE of those who wished to lead a pious life,, the Shaykh laid down ten principles (recorded in the *Ghunyat,* 275-76):

(1) Refrain from speaking ill of those not present. (2) Refrain from being unduly suspicious of others. (3) Avoid gossip and malicious asides (4) Abstain from looking at anything which is prohibited. (5) Always tell the truth. (6) Always be grateful to God. (7) Spend money on those who are deserving of help. (8) Abstain from straining after worldly power and position. (9) Be regular in saying the five daily prayers. (10) Adhere to the *Sunnah* of the Prophet and be cooperative towards Muslims.

The role of the spiritual mentor is underscored by the Shaykh in his explanation of his doctrine of spiritual advancement. In *Futhuh al-ghayb* he compares the spiritual guide to "a wet nurse who feeds the baby". However, in the same work on p.54, he makes the point that the Shaykh is a necessity only in so far as his hearers are consumed by base instincts and desires, and are bent upon achieving unworthy ends. But once the lower cravings have been overcome, the Shaykh is no longer needed. This explanation makes it clear that, in the early stages of one's spiritual endeavours, the guidance of a mentor is essential, but that if one's later career is marked by due progress, one may proceed independently. Once the Shaykh has brought his disciple to the point of turning resolutely away from worldly allurements, he is no longer needed as a spiritual guide.

"The greatest pleasure for people in heaven," remarks the Shaykh, "would be the vision of God" (*Ghunyat,* 321-39).

Shaykh 'Abd al- Qadir urged his followers to desire for others what they desired for themselves and to refrain from wishing for others what they did not wish for themselves (*al-Fath al-rabbani*, 107). He quoted the following aphorism from the Quran: "Surely God loves the doers of good to others" (III, 133) and based upon it the principle that service to mankind is a worthy spiritual deed and that it is a major religious and spiritual duty to make every effort to bring about social welfare. When he equated the "service of mankind" with 'the highest spiritual activity of man", he greatly broadened the scope of such effort. He looked upon all people as "children of God on earth" (*al-Fath al-rabbani*, 19) and considered that true religious dedication was to be found in giving assistance to the indigent. "Whoever fills his stomach while his neighbour starves is weak in his faith." (*al-Fath al-rabbani*, 109). His altruism reaches its zenith when he says that "he would like to close the doors of hell and open those of paradise to all mankind." It is the duty of those who wish to be pious and righteous firstly to refrain from acting oppressively towards others and secondly to carry out their obligations to them in a sympathetic manner. (*Ghunyat*, 295-96). Quoting 'A'ishah, the Prophet's wife, he repeats a saying of the Prophet to the effect that human mistakes and wrongdoing can be thus categorized: (a) sins one commits against oneself—pardonable by God; (b) sins committed against God by entertaining polytheism—unforgivable by God; (c) acts of tyranny carried out against other human beings—God would not forgive even the most trifling of such acts. (*Ghunyat*, 262-63).

Hypocrisy is placed on a parallel with polytheism (*Ghunyat*,

478). Hypocrites will bring down upon themselves God's wrath. Even a scholar *('alim)* who does not live up to his knowledge is branded as a hypocrite. In fact, the Shaykh advised his followers to shun those who did not make proper use of their acquired knowledge. *(at-Fath al-rabbani, 83).* He is particularly vehement against those who are "like lambs in appearance but are really wolves in thought and action." *(Ghunyat, 480)*

He advised his flock to live on what they earned by honest means and by their own efforts, and to share what they earned with others. But he advised them also not to become completely dependant on those from whom they gained their livelihood nor to be too reliant on the arts and crafts by which they earned their living. *(al-Fath al-rabbani, 47, 27, 19, no, 145, 160ff.*

The Shaykh kept strictly away from rulers, holding them to be unjust and exploitative. Any dealings with the powers that be were necessarily abhorred by him as running counter to the true spirit of religion. Although the Abbasid caliphs anxiously sought his blessings, he resolutely discouraged any communion with them. Sultan Sanjar reportedly offered the province of Sistan (in southern Persia) to defray the expenses of his *khanqah,* but he refused the offer, saying: "My face may turn black like the canopy of Sanjar, / If except poverty I desire anything from Sanjar's country."

Despite his critical view of rulers, he believed that a people deserved whatever rulers they had, as it was the outcome of their own character and the way they lead their lives. He used to say: "As you are, so shall be your rulers." He constantly advised the people to reform their own thinking and conduct

so that their rulers should also be virtuous. *(al-Fath al-rabbani,*
51).

Litanies and Rituals of the Qadiri Order

SOME OF THE rituals and litanies of the Qadirih Order, which
came into evidence particularly when it spread throughout
Turkey, Egypt, India, and Africa, have been attributed to
Shaykh 'Abd al-Qadir, while others are clearly subsequent
additions. Particular features of the order in different regions
have at times been represented symbolically. The Turkish Qadiris
adopted as their symbol a green rose. In Egypt the Qadiris
wear white turbans and carry white banners. In Morocco
certain Qadiris vocalize their remembrance of God *(dhikr)*
with a musical accompaniment.. In Tangier, when the Jilalah
make vows, they place white cocks in the *zawiyah.* These are
called *muharrar* and their lives are spared.

When a novitiate enters the order, the Qadiri Shaykh
attaches to his felt cap a rose with eighteen sections, with
Solomon's Seal in the centre. This cap is called *taj* (crown),
and is greatly prized in mystic circles.

Invocation and Contemplation

THE MOST IMPORTANT of the spiritual practices of the Qadiri
Order is *dhikr* (reciting the Name of *Allah).* In its performance,
there are different degrees of intensity and emphasis. There is
dhikr with one stroke, two strokes, three strokes, and four
strokes. *Dhikr* with one stroke means firmly repeating the Name
of *Allah* with a long drawn-out breath, as if from high above,

with all the force of heart and throat, and then returning to normal breathing. A long time has to be spent on repeating this continuously. *Dhikr* with two strokes means sitting as for prayer and invoking the Name of *Allah,* first on the right side of the breast and then on the heart. This is done forcefully and repeatedly without gaps. This is considered to facilitate concentration of the heart and to ward off worry and distraction. *Dhikr* with three strokes is performed sitting cross-legged and repeating the Name of *Allah* first at the right side, then at the left, and the third time on the heart. The third stroke has to be much more intense and also more protracted.. *Dhikr* with four strokes is also performed sitting cross-legged and is done by saying aloud the Name of *Allah* first on the right side, then on the left, the third time toward the heart, and the fourth time in front of the breast. The last stroke is expected to be stronger and carried on for a longer period.

After *dhikr* the Qadiris recommend *pas-i anfas,* which means controlling one's breathing so as to cause the name of *Allah* to circulate in the body in the process of inhaling and exhaling. Next is the *muraqabah* (contemplation). For this one has to focus entirely on some verse of the Quran or Divine Quality and then become completely absorbed in contemplation.

In terms of the saint's own ideas and ideals, some of the rituals engaged in by later followers show local influences and are difficult to explain. For example, the followers of the Qadiri Order in North Africa, who are called *Gilanis,* practice the *khalwah* (spiritual retreat) in their own particular way. Reeds are affixed between piles of stones, with rags attached to them by women, and benzoin and styrax are burnt. Both men and women visit this type of *khalwah* and pray for fulfillment.

An almost unavoidable outcome of such practices was the raising of the saint to the level of a deity by extremists. He is supposed to have observed: "All the saints are under my feet." If such a sentiment were actually voiced by the Shaykh, it could only relate to his elevated spiritual state — without there being any suggestion of his prominence in a saintly hierarchy, as claimed by his later admirers. Even Shaykh 'Abd al-Haqq Muhaddith of Delhi, an otherwise very careful scholar of great acuity, depicts the Shaykh in terms stemming from these far-fetched tales of the saints. The greatness of Shaykh 'Abd al-Qadir lay not in his miracles, but in his "God-conscious" way of life and his total devotion to the overarching ideal of Islamic mysticism: to realize God, to show people the way to God, and to bring happiness to troubled hearts and distracted souls.

Suhrawardi Order

THE SUHRAWARDI ORDER was founded by Shaykh Abu al Najib Suhrawardi (1097-1168), the uncle and spiritual guide of Shaykh Shihabuddin Suhrawardi, a contemporary of Abdul Qadir Jilani, celebrated author of *Awariful Maarif*. This order was established on the subcontinent by Shaykh Bahauddin at the beginning of the nineteenth century.

Shaykh Bahauddin's grandfather, Shaykh Kamaluddin Ali Shah, had migrated from Makkah to Khwarazm in Central Asia. His grandparents came to India and settled there permanently. Bahauddin, a grandson of Abdul Qadir Jilani (1077-1165), was born in 1182. His father died when he was only 12 years old. He received his early education in the town. After memorizing the Quran, he went to Khurasan for further studies and spent several years there. He later left for Bukhara. Here, he benefited from the society of renowned religious scholars and Sufi Shaykhs. Besides completing the course of traditional science from Bukhara, he went to Makkah to perform Hajj. Then he went to Madinah where he stayed for five years, studing Hadith with a distinguished Muhaddith,

Shaykh Kamaluddin Muhammad Yamani. He received a *sanad* a formal authorization from Shaykh Yamani to teach Hadith. From there, he went to Jerusalem to pay visits to the ancient prophets who are buried there. He subsequently visited Baghdad, where he joined the circle of disciples of Shaykh Shihabuddin Suhrawardi, who initiated him into his order and made him his Khalifa on his completion of the course of religious training.

Shaykh Bahauddin was already so receptive to spiritual teachings that he took a mere 17 days to grasp the entire course. He had Khilafat conferred upon him within such a short period that the other disciples felt jealous, for they had not been able to achieve this even after several years of training under the Shaykh. When the Shaykh learnt of this complaint, he told them that Bahauddin brought dry wood which caught fire immediately, whereas they were like green wood which takes time to catch fire. Shaykh Bahauddin was directed by his Shaykh to return to the subcontinent and settle in Multan to spread this message he had received from him.

There was a conflict between the Ulama and the Sufis, so Shaykh Bahauddin was also targeted by Maulana Qutbuddin Kashani.

But he could not place obstacles in his path since the Maulana (Kashani) was supported by Naseeruddin Qabacha. He held the Maulana in great esteem, even building a *madrasa* for him where he used to deliver lectures. The Maulana had no faith in the Sufis so a conflict arose between the two leading personalities. The Maulana even wanted Shaykh Bahauddin to go to the *madrasa* for morning prayers. Finally, the Shaykh surrendered, feeling that the Maulana could not do anything to check his popularity for Shaykh Bahauddin had a fine reputation as a scholar, and people attached great importance to his scholarship. Even people from far-off places like Iran and Khurasan came to him in large numbers. The Shaykh built a large Khanqah containing granaries. Here eminent people, men of religion, scholars, wealthy merchants and intellectuals came to meet him. Meetings took place in which spiritual and theological problems were all discussed. The Shaykh took an interest in political matters, so he invited Sultan Shamshuddin Iltutmish to conquer Multan and add it to the Delhi Sultanate. The Qazi of Multan also joined the Shaykh in this invitation. Both letters fell into the hands of Qabacha. He had the Qazi executed and summoned the Shaykh to his palace. The Shaykh very boldly went to him and sat beside him. Then Qabacha gave him the letter and asked him for an explanation. The Shaykh replied that he had written that letter as he had been divinely inspired and said that Qabacha could take any action, although he had no independent authority to do so. Qabacha was perplexed. Then he ordered food for the Shaykh. Qabacha had ordered for the food for he know that the Shaykh would refuse to have it, for he did not eat anywhere except in his Khanqah.

But the Shaykh did eat the food and thus Qabacha's anger subsided. After Iltutmish succeeded in annexing Multan and Sindh in 1228, relations improved, and he gave Shaykh Bahauddin Zakariya the title of Shaykhul Islam. This was a title conferred on religious dignitaries as an honour. They were also given stipends and lands. They were not obliged to go to the court regularly but they were held to various commitments by the ruler. The Shaykh received additional finance for his Khanqah, but he did not take an active interest in political matters. In April-May 1247, the Mongol, Sul Nuyin besieged the Multan fort, and his services were engaged to negotiate peace. Shaykh Bahauddin had good relations with the Chishti Sufis like Khawaja Qutbuddin Bakhtiar Kaki and Baba Farid. Shaykh Bahauddin laid great stress on performing *namaz* and said that all blessings were the result of performing obligatory prayers. To him, omitting to say obligatory prayers was akin to spiritual death. *Zikr* and supererogatory prayers were assigned a secondary place in his Sufi discipline.

He himself did not keep continuous fasts and had normal food. Sometimes, he also indulged in sama like the Chishti Sufis. Shaykh Shahabuddin felt that meditation and contemplation meant freeing the heart from everything except thoughts of God. One's heart and mind should be pre-occupied with constant recitation of *zikr*. He died on 21st Dec. 1262. He was the most popular Sufi in and around Multan, and because he did not stay away from political issues, the rulers and nobles also turned to him for his blessings and prayers. Moreover, because he was famous for his piety and God-fearing life, he was able to negotiate successfully with the Mongol invaders.

One important feature of his religious order was that he was not against possessing wealth earned by lawful means. After his needs, the needs of his family and the Khanqah, what was left out of the money was used for humanitarian purposes, so that the public benefited. He was criticized for his views on the possession of wealth and property and for his close association with Muslim rulers. But, to him, it was not against Islamic teachings to have wealth earned by honest means. Property and wealth was not declared unlawful by Islam in the Shariah. To him what was condemnable was to neglect the higher spiritual and moral values because of involvement in worldly affairs. So long as material things could be kept far from one's heart, there was no harm in possessing them.

Another point was that these worldly resources had to be spent on righteous purposes. Shaykh Bahauddin was criticised for his relations with the rulers. But he had good relations only with good rulers. Sultan Iltutmish was an honest and capable monarch, so the Shayk supported him. And when the Mongols raided the country, he felt it was his duty to extend his full support to establishing the newly formed Delhi. Mongol raids had become a threat to the peace of even such important cities as Multan and Lahore. Shaykh Bahauddin negotiated sincerely with the Mongol invaders. He worked very hard and in about half a century, the Suhrawardi order was established on the subcontinent and it became one of the leading Sufi orders. By dint of his great struggle, he managed to train a number of Khalifahs who could ramify his mission after him.

Sayyed Nuruddin Mubarak Ghaznavi was an important Khalifa of Shaykh Shahabuddin. The details of his early life are not well known. But when he came to Delhi, he had already earned a reputation and that is why he was appointed Shaykhul Islam by Iltutmish. He was called Mir-e-Dehli (Lord of Delhi) by the people. According to Ziauddin Barni, he often visited the Sultan and he did not hesitate to criticize non-Islamic court customs. He believed that Islam could be protected only when its principles were followed by the rulers, and that a ruler who followed these principles would be raised with prophets and saints on the Day of Judgement. The rulers, he felt, should follow the Islamic customs and see that the commands of the Shariah were observed. Sins, debauchery and adultery should not be tolerated. Offenders should be ruthlessly punished.

The pious should be entrusted with the duty to enforce the Shariah and the officers appointed to carry out this task should be well-versed in both the Shariah and the Tariqa. He was against philosophers. He felt that their teachings should be prohibited in Islamic territories. He believed that justice should be rigorously dispensed and that tyrants should be overthrown. He seems to have been an extremist who could not tolerate anything but orthodox Islam. He even went to the extent of saying that those rulers who did not follow these four principles risked damnation in the Hereafter, and that the prayer and fasting alone was not going to benefit them. A disciple of Shaykh Shahabuddin Suhrawardi, he performed Hajj 12 times. He was in Delhi during the reign of Sultan Iltutmish, during which he was offered the post of Sadrus Sudur, which he accepted. But after two years, he resigned and devoted the rest of his life to spiritual exercises. A less well-known Khalifa was Shaykh Ziauddin Rumi. It was he who initiated Sultan Qutbuddin Mubarak Shah Khalji as a disciple and Khalifah.

Qazi Hamiduddin Nagauri was the most famous Khalifah of Shaykh Shahabuddin Suhrawardi. His father was Ataullah

Mahmood and his first name was Muhammad. The family migrated from Bukhara to Delhi at some point before 1200. Shaykh Hamid was appointed the Qazi of Nagaur and served in this position for 3 years. He did not find this service satisfying to his inner nature. So he left Delhi for Baghdad. It was here that he met Shaykh Shihabuddin Suhrawardi and became his disciple. It was here that he also met Khwaja Qutbuddin Bakhtiar Kaki, who later became a renowned Sufi of the Chishti order. Hamididdin and Qutbuddin became friends. Under the influence of Qutbuddin Bakhtiar Kaki, Hamiduddin started taking an interest in *sama*. When he came to Delhi, he met with stiff opposition from the Ulama on the issue of *sama*. But Hamiduddin's intelligence, coupled with his knowledge of the Islamic sciences, left the Ulama speechless. They could do him no harm. After some time, Qazi Hamiddin left for Madinah, where he stayed for some time then he went to Madinah where he stayed longer, for a period of about three years. From Madinah, he went to a number of towns, meeting different Sufis on the way. Then he reached Delhi. By this time, Khwaja Qubuddin Bakhtiar had already come to Delhi.

Qazi Hamiduddin was a writer. He has a number of works to his credit. *Lawaih* (Flashes of Light) was a very important Sufi textbook, which is no longer available. Even Baba Farid used to teach these books to his disciples. Qazi Hamiduddin explains the relationship between the lover and the beloved, saying that they appear to be two separate identities, but in fact they are identical. What a Sufi has to do is annihilate his ego. The more he succeeded in annihilating, the better would he be able to achieve his goal. He goes on to say that love is the source of everything that exists. That both the lover and beloved mirror each other. In short, the essence of all existent beings is God. *Tawah al Shumus* describes in detail God's names. To him God's greatest name is Huwa or He and he says that Huwa or He indicates His eternal nature—holy and free from decline and fall, and then he explains Huwa by quoting from the Quran (Chapter 112, entitled Al-Ahad (The Unity). Those letters of the Qazi addressed to Baba Farid have been preserved by him.

Shaykh Bahauddin disapproved of the Sufis seeking guidance from a number of different peers. He wanted them to surrender to one rather than many. He attached great importance to supererogatory prayers and *zikr*. He did not fast continuously. He died in 1262 in Multan. His tomb became a centre of pilgrimage.

He was succeeded by his son, Shaykh Sadruddin Arif. He was Shaykh Bahauddin's disciple and son-in-law. His fame spread from Syria to Turkey through his disciples. Shaykh Sadruddin Arif had a number of distinguished disciples like the poet Amir Husain Husaini.

Shaykh Sadruddin Arif's son and successor, Shaykh Ruknuddin Abul Fath, earned great renown. This was during the reign of Sultan Alauddin Khalji (1296-1316) He continued to spread the spiritual message of his mentor during the reign of Sultan Mohd bin Tughlaq as well.

Shaykh Ruknuddin was a great admirer of Shaykh Nizamuddin Awliya. His fame spread far and wide. Although his works are not available, certain of the conversations he had with other Sufis have been recorded by other authors. These show that he did not discourage the possession of wealth. For he felt that as well as mystical enlightenment, wealth and scholarship were essential for the spiritual realization of the Sufis. Although the Chishtis did not agree with him on the issue of possessing wealth, they still had good relations with one another. However, not all of the Suharwardi Sufis believed in the possession of wealth. A number of them led ascetic lives like that of Shaykh Usman Sayyah, a disciple of Shaykh Ruknuddin, who lived in Punjab. He went to perform Hajj pilgrimage without even carrying with him a water pot.

Amiruddin of Nagaur's family had migrated from Bukhara to Delhi. He completed his education in Delhi and was appointed the Qazi of Nagaur. He could not continue in service for more than three years, for it did not appeal to his heightened spiritual sensitivity, so he left for Baghdad where he became a disciple of Shaykh Shahabuddin. He travelled extensively, over almost all of western Asia, as the Sufis used to do. And then he came to Delhi. He was a close friend of Khwaja Qutbuddin Bakhtiar Kaki and he participated in many *sama* sessions with him. The ulama opposed him on this issue. But because of his intelligence, logical explanations and his knowledge of the Islamic sciences, the ulama failed to defeat him.

One of the most important disciples of Shaykh Shahabuddin Suhrawardi was Shaykh Jalaluddin Tabrezi. He established himself in Bengal where he was responsible for spreading Islam. He built his Khanqah at Deva Mahal in northern Bengal. Large numbers of Hindus and Buddhists converted to Islam under his influence. His disciples were possessed of a missionary zeal and in Bengal, where the lower classes were being persecuted by the zamindars, they converted to Islam to find the equality and human brotherhood they had been denied for centuries.

But the Chishtis did not believe in mass-scale conversions. Their efforts were chiefly directed at those who had already accepted Islam in order to turn them into practicing Muslims.

Mahdum Jahanian, Syed Jalaluddin Bukhari grandson of Shaykh Bahauddin Zakariya's disciple. Sultan Mohd bin Tughlaq made him the head of the Khanqah of Sehwan. Sultan Mohammad bin Tughlaq controlled the appointments of the heads of the Sufi Khanqah to keep them under his influence. Makhdum Jahanian also went to perform his Hajj and then he traveled to different parts of the Muslim world. Finally he settled down in Uchch during the reign of Sultan Feroz Tughlaq from clest cheff. Makhdum Jahanian would often come to Delhi. He criticized Indian Muslims for having borrowed religious customs and ceremonies from their Hindu compatriots. Being a great humanist, he even encouraged the Sufis to visit rulers and government officials in order to secure their help for needy people.

His son succeeded him and came to be known by the title of Qutb-e-Alam. Qutb-e-Alam and his disciples worked in Gujarat with great zeal and fervour. Under their leadership, the Suhrawardi order spread in Gujarat. The Shaykh and his disciple, Shaykh Jamali, spread the Suhrawardi order in Delhi. Jamali died in 1536. He travelled extensively to spread his mission. He started his travels with the pilgrimage to Makkah and then, travelling to different places, he came to Herat where he met the celebrate Persian poet, Jami. He discussed various topics with him. Jamali was a poet, the author of several Persian *masnavi* (long narrative poems), in which he dealt with the subject of mystical states. His works, *Siyar al Arifin*, a biography of the Gnostics has much information regarding the Chishtis and Suhrawardis in the 14th Century. The Suhrawardi center was established in Kashmir as well.

Shaykh Abdul Haq was a disciple of Shaykh Sadruddin. According to Shaykh Sadruddin, the Sufis should not concentrate on anything other than God. They should not even set heaven as their goal, for that would amount to a distraction from their constant remembrance of God. He said that no breath should be exhaled or inhaled without *zikr*. For *zikr* was a divine light which alone could remove all darkness. Shaykh Sadruddin died in 1286.

Shaykh Bahauddin Zakariyya had a number of famous disciples. One was Hasan Afghan. The Shaykh was proud of him. He would often say that if God asked him what he had brought with him, he would present Hasan as a gift. Once Hasan Afghan went to a mosque to perform his namaz behind the Imam. When the namaz was over, Hasan went up to the Imam and said to him: "You began the namaz and I followed you. In your thoughts you travelled from here to Delhi, did some shopping and then went to Khurasan and Multan and then back to the mosque. What sort of namaz is this?"

Another famous disciple of Shaykh Bahauddin Zakariyya was Shaykh Fakhruddin Ibrahim. He was known as Iraqi. This was his sobriquet. He had memorized the entire Quran and was able to recite it in a very melodious voice. He had also established a madrasa in Hamadan. Shaykh Bahauddin was so

satisfied with Iraqi's spiritual attainments that he presented
him with his own Khirqa to wear and later gave him his
daughter in marriage. Shaykh Bahauddin appointed him his
Khalifa. But the jealousy of other disciples did not let him live
in peace, so he left for Multan in 1263. Iraqi then travelled to
Makkah to perform Hajj, and later went on to Asia Minor. It
is recorded that he also attended lectures delivered by Shaykh
Sadruddin on *Fusus al Hikam* by Ibn Arabi. He also composed
the treatise titled the *Lama'at* (Flashes of Light). It is an attempt
to explain Ibn Arabi's mystic philosophy in beautiful Persian
prose.

His Khanqah was built by Moinuddin Parwana at Tuqat
in Asia Minor. It became an important centre for Sufi musical
gatherings. After Parwana's death, the Shaykh left for Egypt.
Here, the Sultan became Iraqi's disciple. From Egypt, he
migrated to Syria. He was given a warm welcome in Damascus
by both the Ulama and the Sufis. Iraqi died in November
1289 and was buried near the tomb of Ibn Arabi.

Shaykh Sadruddin Arif, Bahauddin Zakariyya's son, had a
scholar disciple, Amir Husain. He came to Delhi during the
reign of Iltutmiah. One of Amir Husain's works is *Nuzhatul
Arwah* (Delight of Souls). Amin Husain was born at *Ghizr*, a
village in Ghur. He was properly educated. Then after receiving
his education, he went to Multan and became Shaykh
Sadruddin's disciple. He stayed in Multan for many years, then
he went to Herat. By this time, he had become very popular.

He wrote a number of works on Sufism. Nuzhatul Arwah
describes the spiritual faith of pilgrimage. It was written in
mixed prose and verse. It became very popular as a Sufi text.

It deals with knowledge, truth (*maarifah*), Sufism in general and the stages of the path of the *salik*. He very passionately describes divine love. He believes that love is known only to true lovers. And that it is love which differentiates between a believer and an unbeliever. He believed that to lead an ascetic life what was required was complete obliteration of all thoughts relating to anything other than God, whether material or immaterial in nature. Amir Husain took great interest in *sama*. He said that the ulama and the Sufis were the leaders of the community, because of their knowledge of the Shariah and Tariqa and that it was owing to their efforts that people received guidance.

Another Sufi was Maulana Husamuddin, a disciple of Shaykh Sadruddin. He came to Badayun and lived there until his death. He was known as the Maulana of Multan.

Shaykh Ahmad Mashuq was a disciple of Shaykh Sadruddin. He belonged to Qandhar. His father was a merchant. He used to go to Multan with his father on trading journeys. It was there that he met Shaykh Sadruddin.

He gained greatly from his teachings and personality. He received spirituality in his company and became his disciple. He totally withdrew from the world and engrossed himself completely in meditation.

Another well-known disciple of Shaykh Sadruddin was Shaykh Salahuddin Darvish. He was a contemporary of Sultan Muhammad bin Tughlaq. He became the Shaykh's disciple in his youth. Then he migrated to Delhi from Multan and stayed near Shaykh Nasiruddin Chiragh Dilli. But he shunned rulers and officials, unlike Shaykh Nasiruddin.

Shaykh Sadruddin's son, Shaykh Ruknuddin, succeeded him. He was very spiritually sensitive, even when he was just a child. He visited Delhi in the reign of Sultan Alauddin Khalji. The Sultan welcomed him and presented him with a large amount of money but the Shaykh did not keep even a single penny for himself. He also distributed all his possessions among the poor and the needy. The people loved him. Shaykh Ruknuddin held Shaykh Nasiruddin in great respect. He was impressed by his spiritual personality. Sultan Mohd bin Tughlaq and Shaykh Ruknuddin had good relations. The Sultan had also gifted him 100 villages to serve the requirements of the Kanqah. He was given a free hand to spread his mission because of his policy of non-confrontation with the rulers. He was even ready to bless the good rulers and supported them in their good policies.

We learn from Ibn Batutah's travelogue that his fame had reached far and wide through the merchants. It was in fact some trader who had asked to meet Shaykh Ruknuddin during his visit to Delhi. When Ibn Batutah reached Multan in 1333, he stayed with one of the Shaykh's disciples. The Shaykh favoured Ibn Batutah with an audience during which he had discussions with the Shaykh on various topics.

Shaykh Ruknuddin's teachings are not available today in writing. He taught his disciples to lead peaceful lives, shun oppressive ways, and opt for a life free from oppression and greed. His view was that such vices brought human beings to the level of beasts. To him, self-purification was essential for spiritual realization and that self-purification could be attained only through humility and prayer. He believed that purification of the self depended on divine grace, as mentioned in the Quran:

Had it not been for the grace and mercy of God, not one of you would ever have been cleansed of sin. (24:21)

He said that God would bestow His grace only upon one who was humble and who sincerely repented his wrongdoings.

The ideological difference between Chishtis and Suhrawardis was mainly over the issue of the possession of money. The Suharwardis said that if they did not have money, how could they fulfill the needs of the poor and the deprived? But the Chishti Sufis said that money was not necessary. Only knowledge was necessary.

Shaykh Ruknuddin (d. 1334) was succeeded by his grandson, Shaykh Hud. Soon, the Governor of Sindh accused Shaykh Hud of misappropriating the income of the Khanqah. The Sultan gave orders to seize the entire property of the Khanqah. The Shaykh was reduced to a miserable condition and finally the Sultan executed him.

With the execution of Shaykh Hud, Shaykh Bahauddin Zakariyya's Khanqah in Multan no longer remained the centre of Sufi activity. However, the Suharwardi Silsila found other centres in which to spread its wings.

Shaykh Ruknuddin had a disciple by the name of Shaykh Usman Sayyah, the son of Qazi Wajihuddin. Once he happened to meet Shaykh Ruknuddin and was impressed by his personality at the very first meeting. Shaykh Ruknuddin accepted him as his disciple and took him to Multan to give him spiritual training. He was very receptive. He was taught the *Awariful Maarif*, the Sufi manual by the Shaykh and he also memorized the Quran during his stay in the Khanqah.

Shaykh Usman absorbed himself completely in meditation and other spiritual exercises. Ultimately, he became an ascetic in the full sense, possessing nothing but a loincloth. Then, with the permission of the Shaykh, he left for Makkah to perform his Hajj pilgrimage.

From Makkah, he came to Multan but did not stay there for long. Then he left Multan for Delhi. It was the reign of Muhammad bin Tughlaq. The Shaykh advised him to pay frequent visits to Shaykh Nizamuddin. As advised, he would often come and meet Shaykh Nizamuddin. With this association, he developed an interest in *sama*. Although the *Ulama*, as usual, turned against him for his participation in *sama* gatherings, they could not do any harm to him. He continued to live in Delhi till his last days. He died in 1337.

Suhrawardi Ideology and Practice

THE SUHRAWARDI AND Chishti traditions were not opposed to one another, one main reason being that the book, *Awarifu Maarif*, was the only textbook used by all the Sufis. Although the early Chishti Sufis were scholars, they did not write a book which might have served as a Sufi textbook. Another Suharawardi Sufi, Qazi Hamuddin Nagauri, also wrote number of books, which were read with interest by the Sufi of different orders.

The Jamaat Khana, or hostel accommodation, for the dervish was an important part of the shrine. The Jamaat Khana also had assembly hall, as it was essential for conducting meditation and other spiritual exercises.

The Suharwardis built Khanqahs, with the help of grant

for they accepted gifts from rulers, and merchants. They had thus no dearth of money and had abundant food in the Khanqah. Shaykh Bahauddin Zakariyya did not tolerate *qalandars,* for he believed that everyone should work and make money instead of opting for a life of dependency on others. But Shaykh Ruknuddin was more tolerant. He felt that it was the demand of the *qalandars* and dervishes that justified the Shaykhs in keeping money.

The culture in the Chishti Jamaat Khana was somewhat different from that of the Suhrawardi. Here, everyone was welcome. It was open for all. Even if there was nothing in the Jamaat Khana to offer to the visitor, a glass of water would be presented with apologies. For they believed, in the full sense in the equality and brotherhood of man. They were all one and the same, all were God's creatures in equal measure. In this ideology, there was no room for discrimination between one and another. They were all God's servants, seekers of truth and deserving of respect.

The concept of *Wahdatul Wajud* had not taken root in the early Chishti or Suharwardi Sufis.

In the fourteenth century, these ideas of Ibn Arabi were introduced into India by Iraqi, the Suhrawardi Sufi. *Awaraful Maarif,* which served as a sufi classic also dealt with the theme of *waadatul wajud*—the oneness of existence. This experience, which the *Sufis* claimed to have had, was based on the notion that the "lover, love and beloved were all one"—that life with God rested entirely on love. However, at that time these ideas had not been fully developed. The mystic had such experiences while in a state of ecstasy. That is why they gave great importance to ecstatic experiences, even at the cost of great opposition from the orthodox Ulamas. To induce ecstasy the music of *sama* was essential. But the Ulama's stand was that music was not lawful in Islam. Then how could an experience be beneficial which was arrived at by unlawful means.

Each entrant to the Sufi path was required to begin his spiritual course with *tauba* (repentance). This was done under the guidance of the *pir*. The *salik* was asked to submit to the divine will. The two orders differed to some extent as regards the details of the rituals.

The Suharwardis attached great importance to *salat* (prayer) and *zikr* (remembrance of God) so far as the purification of the soul was concerned. They believed that fasting in the month of Ramazan was sufficient for this purpose. This annual training course, if performed properly, would suffice for the whole year. Shaykh Bahauddin Zakaria recited this verse of the Quran to his followers: "Eat what is pure and act righteously."

The advice Shaykh Jalaluddin Tabrizi gave to his followers is very interesting: "Eat three times a day and use the strength gained from the food for prayers and abstention from sin." (*Fuwaidul Fuwad*, p. 226)

But the Chishtis believed in rigorous ascetic exercise. They gave great emphasis to fasting to achieve the goal of spiritual purification. They often fasted on alternate days. Even when they ate, they ate very little. Self-mortification, meditation and contemplation formed an essential part of the Chishti life.

They had learnt different techniques, particularly of exhalation and inhalation from the yogis. They employed all these yoga techniques to achieve concentration, which was essential to the enhancement of mystical sensitivity. *Sama* formed an indispensable part of the Chishti rituals. The Suhrawardis did not attach such importance to *sama* but they too indulged in it on occasion.

The Suhrawardi order was closer to the spirit of Islam. These Sufis were more orthodox and played an important part in the preservation of the classical Sufi doctrine than to the philosophy of *wahdatul wajud*, propagated by Ibn Arabi. They did not preach the renunciation of the world like the Chishtis. They laid great emphasis on the recitation of *zikr* and the prescribed fasting in the month of Ramzan. They also rejected the practice of self-prostration before the Shaykh adopted by the Chishtis. Neither did they take much interest in *sama*. They could not reject it altogether, allowing it only for the *salik* at an advanced stage.

Naqshbandi Order-1

KHWAJA BAHAUDDIN NAQSHBAND (1317-1389), the founder of the Naqshbandi order, was born at Kushk-I-Hinduwan, a village near Bukhara. This village later came to be known as Kushk-I-Arifaan. The title of Naqshband literally means a painter or embroiderer. This title may refer to his family profession, if his ancestors were embroiderers. Otherwise, it is indicative of his spiritual capacity to leave the imprint of the name of God upon a disciple's heart.

In his times it was not uncommon to send children to the Sufis to receive spiritual knowledge. But it was only after receiving education in orthodox disciplines like the Quran, Hadith and jurisprudence that they were sent to the Sufis.

At the age of 18 Khwaja Bahauddin was sent to Mohd Baba As Samasi, a Sufi saint, who lived in a village called Sammas. Khwaja Bahauddin had a great aptitude for spirituality. Very soon he had learnt all the spiritual exercises and the Shaykh was very pleased with his receptivity he appointed Naqshband as his representative (khalifa).

Endowed with a keen critical faculty, he did not accept

anything without first applying his mind to it. It is recorded that he disapproved of the loud chanting (*zikr bil jehr*) of God's name. He preferred silent chanting. In those days, it was considered a taboo in the world of Sufism to criticize the mentor's method of training. Nevertheless, he boldly expressed his views. But Samasi's disciples were not ready to change their ways. Finally, the Shaykh, as-Samasi himself, declared it openly that his disciple, Bahauddin Naqshband, was right. How bold it was on his part to accept his own disciple's views publicly. And not only did he give his approval.

After his mentor's death he left Sammas for Samarqand and then went on to Bukhara and a number of other towns. The Sufis used to renounce worldly life in search of truth and spirituality. This spirituality which they were looking for was, of course, to be found in books. And books were certainly of great value, for they prepared one to become receptive to truth and spirituality. But even so, they always went from place to place in search of realized souls in order to learn from their spiritual experiences.

The Sufis believe that spirituality is transferred from heart to heart, but the owner of the heart must have the quality of receptivity. Otherwise he or she will not be able to appreciate what is being offered in terms of spirituality. The same was true of Bahauddin. He went from one place to another in search of realized souls who could show him the spiritual path. Such spiritual journeys are facilitated by the fact that these seekers have no worldly possessions to present any obstacle to their search.

There was a Sufi called Amir Kulal at Nasaf. Bahauddin

stayed there for some time and took spiritual lessons from him. After his death he spent some time with his successor, Arif al Dikkirani.

After the death of his mentor, As Samasi, he went to Bukhara, where he got married. In the course of his mystic training he also grazed herds of animals for several years. The purpose of this training was to build up a sense of service, and awaken those feelings of love and compassion and philanthropy, which were considered necessary for the seeker. The last years of his life were spent in his own home town near Bukhara. He died in his native village in 1389. This order, by the time of Khwaja Bahauddin, had undergone several stages on the way to perfection and was also known as Silsila-e-Khwajgan. It is said to have initially started with the first caliph, Abu Bakr, and another senior companion of the Prophet, Salman Farsi. It was Khwaja Bahauddin, however, who popularized this spiritual order in central Asia, attracting people to it from all walks of life. It is on record that he had meetings with certain rulers and nobles, but as a general principle he avoided contacts with them as far as possible. The main reason for this was that he was very particular about his income being lawful.. And he did not trust the ruling class in this regard. That is why he refrained from mixing with them or partaking of food with them.

The Khwaja lived a very simple life. When asked why he did so, he replied: "Ownership does not go with the mystic path." —the reason being that the moment one had worldly objects in one's possession, one's heart became attached to them. This was the biggest obstacle to reaching out to God or Truth.

The same view is held by men of religion in Hinduism, Buddhism and Jainism. They believe that the heart cannot simultaneously concentrate on two such aspects of life as are diametrically opposed to each other. If we want to discover Truth, or God for that matter, we shall have to be content with the bare necessities, so that there may be no hindrance in our path.

Khwaja Bahauddin believed that without holding fast to the ways of the Prophet and his companions, that is, to the path of the Shariah, one could not attain the realization of God. Obviously, realization of God can be attained only by treading the path shown by HIm through His prophets.

He took a great interest in the training and education of his disciples in spirituality. Often the disciples were converts from other faiths, so they needed greater attention, having no knowledge of the Islamic faith. He spared no effort in training them thoroughly in order that they might communicate the message to the uninitiated.

According to Shah Waliullah, in laying down such a rigorous and exacting discipline for his disciples, Khwaja Bahauddin was influenced by his Turkish background.

The Pioneers of the order

THIS ORDER IS also known as the Khwajagan order, for a number of important personalities like Khwajah Yusuf Hamadani (d. 1140), his successor Khwaja Abdullah Barqi, Khwaja Hasan Andaqi, Khwaja Ahmad Yisiwi, and Khwaja Abd al Khaliq Ghujdawani were associated with it. They played a very great role in its popularization. In so far as the organization of the order was concerned, it resulted mainly from the efforts of Khwaja Bahauddin Ahmad, who had received his famous 8-fold spiritual doctrine under the guidance of his mentor, Abdul Khaliq of Ghujdwan.

Abdul Khaliq laid great emphasis on the observance of the injunctions of the Quran and Sunnah. He also discouraged his disciples from associating themselves with kings and rulers.

Khwaja Abdul Khaliq (d. 1179) born at Ghujdwan in Uzbekistan, expressed his mystical thoughts in his treatises: *Risala-yi-tariqat* (Treatise on the Spiritual Path), *Nasihat-namah* (Treatise of Advice) and *Risala-i-Sahibiyyah* (The Sahibiyya Treatise).

His spiritual will (*Nasihat-namah*) gives the following instructions to his disciples:

Familiarize yourselves with Islamic jurisprudence (*fiqh*) and the traditions of the Prophet (*ahadith*). Do not consort with mystics who are illiterate. Say your prayers in congregation. Do not crave renown. Reject any offers of official positions. Neither stand surety for anyone nor be yourself litigious. Avoid the company of rulers and princes Do not construct a *khanqah*. Turn a deaf ear to too much mystic music, but do not condemn it entirely. Eat only what is lawful. To the extent possible, do not marry a woman who hankers after the comforts and convenience of a worldly life. Laughter corrodes the heart. Your heart should be grief- stricken, your body like that of a sick man, and your eyes filled with tears. You should be sincere in whatever you do, particularly in saying your prayers. You should dress in threadbare clothing and keep company with dervishes. Your only wealth should be your poverty, your home should be the mosque and God should be your friend. 31(*Rashahat*)

Khwaja Ghujdawani's greatest contribution to the order was that he consolidated the thoughts of the earlier saints in the form of aphorisms which came to form the basis of this order.

There were eight main principles to be observed by the disciples. They are as follows:

1. *hush dar dam:* The Sufi, while breathing in and out, must remember God in a state of total awareness, for he should never ventilate his lungs without giving proper thought to what he does.

2. *Nazar bar qadam:* A Salik (one who treads the Sufis' spiritual path) must evaluate all of his own actions, for every move he makes should be in the direction of fulfilling some divine purpose.

3. *safar dar watan:* introspection, that is, the practice of scrutinizing one's inner self in order to fully appreciate the state of one's own psyche.

4. *khalwat dar anjuman:* solitariness when with others, that is, engaging externally with one's fellow men, yet all the while remaining internally alone in spiritual conclave with the Almighty.

5. *yad kard:* remembrance.

6. *baz gard:* keeping one's thinking under constraints.

7. *nigah dash:* being vigilant about the shape one's thinking is taking.

8. *yad dash:* cherishing the Almighty by focusing one's full attention on His remembrance.

The saints who followed 'Abd al-Khaliq Ghujdawani developed a whole philosophy of mystic discipline based on these aphorisms. They also added the following three concepts to it;

9. *wuquf-i 'adadi:* being vigilant about recalling God, so that one's attention is not diverted..

10. *wuquf-i zamani:* taking stock of one's activities, while showing gratitude to God for the time devoted to virtuous deeds, and repenting one's misdeeds.

11. *wuquf-i qalbi:* keeping the heart alive and receptive to God's messages. .

These practices were designed to regulate man's whole inner existence. They gave clear expression to spiritual experiences, and defined the spiritual states passed through by the mystic while on his spiritual quest..

There were certain other important figures of the order like Khwaja Ali Ramitini, who was called by his devotees Hadrat-I-aizan. Khwaja Ali practiced *zikr* in a loud voice. When asked about this, he replied that a beginner is supposed to do the repetition of the Name of Allah loudly, but advanced mystics could do it in their hearts, that is, by silent repetition.

Khwaja Ali's dedication to the mission is evident from the way he worked to disseminate the teachings of his order. At Khwarazm he used to go out daily to the labour market and engage some labourers. First of all he would he explain to them about Islamic hygiene and then he would instruct them in how to say their prayers and the proper way to engage in other forms of worship. Afterwards he would ask them to do *zikr* all the time, even when they were engaged in practical matters. Then, at the end of the day, after having given them religious and spiritual education throughout the day, he would give them their wages and let them go home. He kept up this practice for a long period of time until he died in Khwarazm. His ceaseless efforts succeeded in bringing about a spiritual revolution in the region.

Disciples of Khwaja Naqshband

KHWAJA ALAUDDIN AND Khwaja Muhammad Parsa were the most noteworthy disciples of Khwaja Naqshband. Khwaja Attar took a very active part in training the new converts to the order. His method of spiritual instruction was very appealing. Along with Khwaja Parsa, he made a concerted effort to put the Naqshbandi doctrine into practice. Their main emphasis was on making lawful earnings, cultivation being preferable to trade. They attached the utmost importance to the tradition of personal labour. being the best way of earning a livelihood in the eyes of God.

Khwaja Muhammad Parsa (d. 1419) was a great Sufi of the time. One can gauge his spiritual heights from this saying which he often repeated : "One should always pray to God with the same fear and faith with which a dying person turns to Him in supplication." Only a realized soul can utter such words. It is indeed true that our supplications can be heard by God only when they are made in all sincerity. Thanks to his scholarship and piety, Khwaja Parsa was accorded great respect by the princes in central Asia.

A number of the Naqshbandi Sufis were original thinkers. We find among them commentators of the Quran. In their commentaries they highlighted the spiritual aspect of the scriptures, making a special point of explaining those verses which concerned spiritual truths. Their aim in writing commentaries was very commendable. They wanted to arouse people's interest in a study of the Quran, the basic source of Islam.

Khwaja Ubaydullah Ahrar (1403-1490) is regarded as the most powerful Sufi Shaykh of the order. He was born at Shash (Tashkand) to a poor family. His father, Khwaja Mahmud Shaashi, was a poor farmer and his family saw very hard times. . During winter they did not have enough clothing to keep themselves warm. He always remembered his difficult days, and this perhaps accounts for his great concern for the poor and the destitute.

He did not show any interest in receiving formal education. One of his maternal uncles, Khwajah Ibrahim, was keen on having him educated, but he did not succeed in his efforts

It is also reported that Khwaja Ahrar, as we have mentioned earlier, believed in manual labour. He himself set an example of earning a living in this way. After he returned from his spiritual journeys, he would engage in cultivation and would plough the fields himself.. He worked so hard that very soon his economic condition improved to the extent that he was able to purchase 33 hundred villages, including the famous village known as Pashaghar.

Of all the Naqshbandi saints he was the wealthiest. But his wealth did not make him vain. In fact, he regarded pride and arrogance as the worst moral evils. He was very modest and had an extremely humane temperament. He believed that a

mystic could not indulge in pride and arrogance, as these evils
were totally against the leading of a spiritual life.

Khwaja Ahrar was a humanist par excellence. Regarding
service to humanity to be of supreme spiritual value, he spared
no effort in helping the poor and the downtrodden. Without
doubt his love and affection for the people won the hearts of
the high and low alike. Even Babar held him in high esteem
and considered him a source of spiritual guidance.

Once during Khwaja's stay in Samarqand, an epidemic
broke out. Khwaja himself attended on the patients, even
washing their soiled beds. He used to say: "People have reached
their spiritual goals through different gates. In my case it has
been through the door of service to mankind." He said that
those who did not come to people's assistance were as good as
tyrants. He said, moreover, that not only other human beings
but also animals deserved sympathy.

Khwaja Ahrar measures up to the highest ideals of human
behaviour. In spite of possessing so much wealth, his heart was
not attached to worldly things. He believed in contentment
which brought peace of mind, and, without doubt, peace of
mind was essential for the spiritual discipline that the Khwaja
stood for.

Khwaja laid the greatest emphasis on the remembrance of
God at all times. What is significant in this spiritual discipline
presented by the Khwaja is that he did not demand that a
person cut himself off completely from society and meditate in
seclusion, as had formerly been the practice in other religious
disciplines. It is a truly Islamic concept that a believer, even
while attending to all the routine work of life, will have his

heart set on the remembrance of God. This discipline requires the development of such an attitude of mind that, even when one is engaged in worldly activities, one remains preoccupied with the remembrance of God. He would say that *dhikr* was not just the soulless utterance of certain phrases, but something that should permeate one's whole being He believed that the remembrance of God was the life of the heart. He used to advise his disciples to remain engrossed in thoughts of God at all times, because it was necessary for spiritual development. He did not like the company of those who had no interest in spirituality.

Khwaja Ahrar emphasized cleanliness. He said that if the mystics dressed shabbily, they would not be able to attract people to their cause.

Naqshbandi Order-2

IN ALL THE spiritual orders a *salik*, i.e. a sufi under training, is supposed to have full faith in his guide. It is a sine qua non in the mystic discipline. Similarly Khwaja too wanted his followers to have full faith in their spiritual guide, for lack of faith would have become an obstacle to their spiritual development.

Khwaja's views on celibacy

ALTHOUGH KHWAJA WAS not against married life per se, he felt that it was preferable for mystics to remain single, for married life was a great distraction. He believed that prophets could marry because their concentration level was very high, so they did not incur the risk of being distracted. So far as the common man was concerned, Khwaja held that they did not require such a high level of concentration, hence marriage did not pose a problem for them. It was for mystics that he thought celibacy was preferable. He once observed, that a single breath that one draws from inside with the remembrance of God was better than seventy two thousand sons.

To Khwaja, concentration and meditation had to be aimed

at subordinating all one's actions to God's will. God should be forever present in one's thoughts. For him mental concentration was more important for a mystic in the facilitation of his spiritual journey than spontaneous spiritual states like *hall* (ecstasy, rapturous states), because mental concentration was an abiding thing, while ecstasy was a fleeting experience.

Like Rabia Basri, he also enjoined upon his disciples that they should worship God for His love alone, and not for the fear of hell.

In one point the Naqshbandi order was different from other orders. The Naqshbandi shaykhs in most cases, held that the rulers should not be avoided. They should be kept in touch with in order to exert a healthy influence on them. And he believed that only through their reform could Muslims be protected from their tyranny. So the rulers, to their way of thinking could be positively influenced by approaching them rather than by keeping away from them. Khwaja Ahrar had good relations with many princes of the time, amongst whom were Yunus Khan, Sultan Ahmad Mirza, and Umar Shaykh Mirza. The last mentioned, Babar's father, was in fact his disciple. Babar has mentioned in his *Babar Nama* the positive influence Khwaja had on his father. Such saints played an important role in the medieval world because of the respect and honour in which they were held by the people, and they were often invited to act as arbitrators in serious conflicts. People, being mostly religious-minded, lost no time in adopting them as their leaders and guides in both religious and secular matters. Interestingly, they approached them not only for their spiritual but also for their physical health. These Sufis kept their doors open to all and sundry. The lowliest and the highest could equally expect their maximum attention.

Khwaja Ahrar wrote only one book — actually at insistence of his father, Khwaja Mahmud Shashi — entitled *Risala-e-Walidiyyah* (Treatise Presented to the Father). He was held in such high esteem by Babar that the latter himself rendered this Persian treatise into Turkish verse. Babar was ill at that time, but he believed that working on this treatise would have a healing effect on him and he would recover from his illness.

Abdur Rahman Jami

MAWLANA ABDUR RAHMAN Jami (1414-1492), born in the town of Jam in Khurasan, was one of those Sufis who had the opportunity to complete his education in traditional learning. Due to his spiritual inclinations, he felt less than satisfied with the formal education of the madrasas. He knew that the Sufis taught important books of *tasawwuf* to those of their select disciples, who showed a greater capacity to grasp the deeper meanings. Therefore, he approached a sufi saint, Khwaja Said al-Din Kashghari (d. 1459) a Khalifah of Khwajah Bahauddin Naqshband, to give him spiritual training. He remained under his guidance for several years. After the death of Khwaja Said Jami, he became a disciple of Khwajah Ubaydullah Ahrar, who taught him Ibn Arabi's al-*Futuhat al Makkiyah* (Makkan Revelations). As a sign of respect, Jami titled one of his Mathawis '*Tuhfat-ul-Ahrar* (Present to Ahrar). Khwajah Ahrar for his part was highly appreciative of his disciple's spiritual attainments. So when Mawlana Jami sent any of his own disciples to Khwaja Ahrar, the latter discouraged this, saying that there was simply no need to take this trouble, for after Mawlana Jami's training, there was no need for them to go anywhere else for this purpose.

Jami's book *Nafahaat al-uns* (Breath of Familiarity) was one of his great contributions to the field of tas*awwuf.* This book not only preserved the life and teachings of many saints of Central Asia and Persia, but also set an example for other writers. . Soon after followed another important book written by Kashifi titled *Rashahat* (Sprinklings) which recorded the history of the Naqshbandi Order.

Professor Browne has summed up his teachings in these words: "The mystical and pantheistic thought of Persia may be said to have found its most complete and vivid expression in him."

Jami was endowed with a deeply aesthetic temperament. This is perhaps the reason why he conceived God as Eternal Beauty. There is a hadith to this effect: "I (God) was a hidden treasure and I desired to become known; therefore I brought creation into being in order that I might be known." To Jami, the purpose of creation was to manifest the Beauty of God. Since God was Eternal Beauty, the human soul's craving for beauty was a means to link the soul to God. Ephemeral beauty thus provided the bridge to Real Beauty.

Jami believed that a mystic might develop himself spiritually only through divine love. He seemed to believe that the love of some human being (*ishq-i-majazi*) helped the mystic in developing the love of God (*ishq-e-haqiqi*). Once the mystic was in the grip of human love, with all the emotions awakened, it was easier for the guide to divert these emotions towards *ishq-e-haqiqi*, that is, to God. Whereas in a case where one was not so charged with emotions, it was difficult for anyone to direct his total concentration to God. For such a person is engrossed with the world at so many points, that severing his connections at so many points is difficult to do. While one who is in love, is focused, and has full concentration at one point.

Taking this concept too far is not without risk, for it may invite freedom from such laws of the shariah as are necessary to bind society together. Perhaps Jami himself had realized this danger in his later days and had withdrawn from these views.

Khwaja Baqi Billah

THE INDIAN SCENARIO. By the sixteenth century the activities of the Naqshbandi order began spreading across the Indian subcontinent, where people seemed very receptive to its ideas. The order was brought to India by Khwaja Baqi Billah, who was seventh in the line of succession from Khwaja Bahauddin Naqshband, its founder. Baqi was born in Kabul, and before coming to India, he undertook a long spiritual journey, as the Sufis used to do, through Transoxania, Samarqand, Bukhara, Kashmir, etc. He found the Indian soil very fertile for sowing the seeds of this spiritual order.

Khwaja Baqi Billah had received full training in the principles of the order under different shaykhs. and proved himself to be a great organizer. It is amazing that, within a short span of four to five years, he managed to establish this order on so firm a footing that since then it has gone on spreading without any break.

Guided by the principles of Khwaja Ubaydullah Ahrar, he also paid equal attention to the common man and the nobles. This approach had a two- fold benefit. Firstly, by bringing the rulers close to the spirit of religion, along with reforming themselves, they would become better rulers, which would in turn benefit the common man. Secondly, the rulers would then support the religious and spiritual leaders and thus the latter would be able to work more effectively. It was in such terms that he conveyed the message of the order to all – to religious scholars, spiritual leaders, government officials and nobles. His efforts succeeded to such a great extent that he attracted such talented disciples as Nawab Murtaza Khan, a political figure, Shaykh Ahmad Sirhindi, a sufi and Shaykh Abdul Haqq, a religious scholar. These were men of great calibre.

Khwaja Baqi Billah had a pleasing personality and people flocked to him, for they found in him their sincere well-wisher. They found peace and spirituality in his company. He was in short the best guide, laying the utmost stress on the purification of the self, which was a pre-requisite for developing a spiritual personality.

Khwaja, like other Sufis, ran a big Khanqah, where the trainees were allowed to stay. There they received not only food but also a stipend for the needy. But to others, who were not Sufis under training, hospitality was extended for only three days. Khwaja believed that a lawful source of earning one's livelihood and faith in the spiritual guide were necessary conditions for imparting to them spiritual training.

Khwaja Baqi Billah believed in the doctrine of *wahdat al-*

wajud, oneness of being, as propounded by Ibn Arabi. However, Shaykh Ahmad Sirhindi, the most famous khalifa (representative) of the Khwaja, did not accept this theory.

Khwaja Baqi Billah laid the greatest of emphasis on purity of character. For him *tasawwuf* consisted of a high standard of character. That is why he exerted his utmost for the purification of the soul. His speech and conversations were so eloquent that people were moved by his words and, within a period of just 3-4 years, a large number of them entered his fold.

At the early age of 40, Khwaja Baqi Billah breathed his last, after successfully launching this spiritual movement in India. Indeed, the achievements of the Khwaja during such a short period of time are spell- binding. Moreover, he left behind him such worthy successors as could make full use of the opportunities he had created for the spread of this order.

Khwaja Ubaydullh, the eldest son of Khwaja Baqi Billah, popularly known as Khwaja Kalan, wrote a book titled *Mablagh al Rijal* (Perfection of Men), which dealt with religious sects in India and Persia. Khwaja Khurd, a younger son, wrote a treatise titled *Talim-i-Salik*. (Instruction of the Traveller upon the Path). This book contained guidelines for entrants to the sufi path. He was taught books on *tasawwuf* by Shaykh Ahmad Sirhindi, the most eminent disciple of Khwaja Baqi Billah.

Khwaja Hisamuddin

BORN IN 1570 in a town called Qandoz to one of Akbar's courtiers, Qazi Nizamuddin Badakhshi, Kwaja Hisamuddin grew up in the midst of worldly luxuries. But, following his heart, he stayed away from all these attractions, for he was of a spiritual disposition. He often visited Sufis during his stay in the Deccan. Finally he decided to renounce the world in favour of a life of spirituality. So he went to Delhi to Khwaja Baqi Billah, became his disciple and lived with his mentor till his last breath. He eventually ranked with such notable disciples as Shaykh Tajuddin Sambhali, Khwaja Mohd Noor, Mirza Hesamuddin Ahmad, and Shaykh Allah Dad.

Khwaja Kalan, Baqi Billah's son, writes in his biography of Khwaja Hisamuddin, that he preferred a life of seclusion and did not like to meet the nobles and rich men, unless there was some real need to do so. Having cultivated a small garden adjacent to the tomb of Khwaja Baqi Billah, he would spend most of his time there, praying, reciting the Quran and in meditation. He died in 1633 in Agra, but was buried in Delhi by the side of his pir.

Shaykh Tajuddin Sambhali

SHAYKH TAJUDDIN SAMBHALI was perhaps the first disciple of Khwaja Baqi Billah, having entered his fold during his visit to Sambhal. After Baqi Billah's death, Tajuddin went to Arabia, where he spent most of his time. He also stayed for some time in Egypt. He spread this order far and wide in both Arabia and Egypt. He also wrote a number of books and translated several books from Arabic.

Shaykh Tajuddin enjoyed great success. This was because Shaykh Mohd Allan, who was associated with Haram (the Kabah), was already interested in the Naqshbandi order and became his disciple. Even the Governor of Basra came under his influence. Shaykh Tajuddin ultimately bought a tract of land near Haram and stayed there for the rest of his life. He died in 1052 A.H. at the age of 99 and was buried in Makkah.

Shaykh Abdul Haq Muhaddith

SHAYKH ABDUL HAQ Muhaddith of Delhi was one of the most eminent disciples of Khwaja Baqi Billah. Basically an academician, he concentrated on academic work. Having developed a special interest in the traditions of the Prophet, he devoted his entire life to propagating the authentic traditions. He not only taught at the seminary, but also wrote about sixty books on a number of religious themes.

Another important contribution he made to the history of Sufism is his biographical dictionary of the Indian Sufis, titled: *'Akhbar al-Akhyar* (Annals of Pious Men).

Shaykh Ahmad Sirhindi

SHAYKH AHMAD SIRHINDI earned more renown than any of the other disciples so far as the propagation and establishment of the Naqshbandi order in India was concerned. Born in 1563 in Sirhind, a town in Punjab, he was the son of Shaykh Abdul Ahad Makhdum. Shaykh. Abdul Ahad, being a man of religion, was fond of the company of devout Muslims. He was, moreover, a religious scholar, and taught his students not only the Quran, hadith and, *fiqh*, but also books of *tasawwuf.* He followed the teachings of the Prophet to the letter. That is why he developed an interest in the Naqshbandi order, for they strictly adhered to the teachings of the Quran and Sunnah. So it was but natural that Shaykh Ahmad should inherit this interest from his father. In his early childhood he was given a proper religious education. First of all, he learnt the Quran by heart. Then he was taught by his father at home. After learning the languages and basic knowledge of the religious sciences, he was sent to Sialkot to receive education under the guidance of Kamal Kashmiri. Yaqub Kashmiri, a great scholar of Hadith, was his hadith teacher. By the age of 17 he had studied all the necessary courses in religious education and had himself started teaching. Later, he went to Agra for further studies. There he met Abul Fazl and Faydi, who were held in great esteem at the court of Akbar. Soon after he married the daughter of a noble named Shaikh Sultan of Thanesar.

At the age of twenty eight, after the death of his father, whose training had been responsible for developing his spirituality, he went to Delhi and visited Khwaja Baqi Billah. By that time too he had also been introduced to the Qadriyah and Chishtiya schools of mysticism. The Khwaja, on seeing the Shaykh, understood his spiritual potential and took great interest in him. The Shaykh too realized Khwaja's spiritual attainments. Shaykh Ahmad then decided to become his disciple. Khwaja focused his full attention on him, so that the Shaykh did not take more than a few months to complete his training in the Naqshbandi order.

Naqshbandi Order-3

KHWAJA BAQI BILLIAH appointed Shaykh Ahmad his vicegerent (Khalifa) and sent him to Sirhind. He gave him a *khirqa* (gown) as a symbol of his having completed his training in spiritual knowledge. When Shayk Ahmad went back to Sirhind, he started disseminating his knowledge to others. He devoted himself fully to the cause of God, guiding and reforming his fellow men to the best of his ability. For this purpose, he built a mosque and a large house (*haveli*).

He chose different ways of communicating his message to others — through conversation, meetings, sermons, letters, books, etc. By his time, because of the degeneration of the Muslims and because of free mixing with non-Muslims, a number of un-Islamic practices had gradually taken hold in Muslim society, such as observing religion only in the letter and not in the spirit. Four years later, he paid another visit to Khwaja Baqi Billah and was received by the Shaykh with great respect and honour. His mystical dispositions were listened to with great appreciation by the Khwaja . After some time he went back to Sirhind. By now his fame had spread far and wide and his spiritual attainments were recognized even by the Qadria order. He had a *khirqa* bestowed upon him by Sayyid Sikandar Qadiri, a descendant of Abdul Qadir Gilani. This giving of recognition to the spiritual attainment of anyone associated with another order was an extraordinary gesture on the part of the Qadri order.

In 1603-04 Shaykh Ahmad paid his third visit to his *pir* (Shaykh), Khwaja Baqi Billah, who on this occasion gave him even greater recognition. The Khwaja went so far as to say, "Ahmad has guided us to the true interpretation of Sufi pantheism. In the knowledge of mysticism he is like the sun, while we are like the planets revolving around him."

Soon after the death of Khwaja Baqi Billah, Shaykh Ahmad was acknowledged by the Khwaja's followers as the head of the Naqshbandi order. People in general regarded him as a m*ujaddid,* a reformer of Islam. That is why this order came to be known as the Naqshbandiya—Mujaddadiya.

Shaykh Ahmad had become very popular among all classes of people. In his times numerous heresies, as well as Akbar's man-made religion, Din-E-Ilahi, had spread among the Muslims. Shaykh Ahmad made it his mission to purge Islam of all such heresies as had gained ground with his Muslim contemporaries.

During Jahangir's rule, the Shias had gained great influence. Asif Jah, a Shia, Noor Jahan's brother, was the Prime Minister. He was enraged by Shaykh Ahmad's religious movement on two counts, one, Ahmad's success in bringing leading court officials into his fold and, second, his combating Shia influence in the State through his writings . One of his

works was titled *Radd-e-Rawafiz* (Rejection of Shia Heretical
Tenets). Shaykh Ahmad's goal was, in effect, to restore Sunni
Islam to its pristine state. That was why he was hailed by the
orthodox as the saviour of Islam. When his influence began to
have a serious effect on the court, Asif Jah determined to nip
this new movement in the bud. He succeeded in convincing
the emperor that it was very dangerous to the state.

Kings never tolerate the rise of any popular movement
and Jahangir was no exception. On the advice of Asif Jah, the
first step he took was to transfer the court officials who had
come under the influence of Shaykh Ahmad. Of these Khan-
i-Khanan was sent to Daccan; Sayyed Sadar Jahan to Bengal;
Khan-i-Jahan to Malwa and Mahabat Khan to Kabul. Once
the court was cleared of his supporters, he was summoned to
the court, where he presented himself along with some of his
followers. When he came into the presence of the Emperor
Jahangir, he refused to bow before him. When he was urged
to observe the court etiquette, he replied that it was against
the tenets of Islam to bow one's head to any of God's creatures.
This audacity in the presence of the Emperor resulted in his
imprisonment in the Fort of Gwalior.

Shaykh Ahmad was released from imprisonment after one
year. Then Jahangir asked him to remain in the custody of the
army for another two years. Being a missionary, he exploited
every opportunity to introduce to his fellow detainees the true
picture of Islam. A number of non-Muslims converted to Islam
under his guidance.

For three or four years he travelled extensively along with
the army, during which period he continued his *dawah*

activities. He continued, for example, to write letters to a number of different people, which were intended to bring them closer to the real face of Islam. These letters show his great concern for the revival of the faith. He believed that, solely by following the Sunnah, it was possible for us to share in God's blessings in this world as well as in the Hereafter. By the grace of God, he succeeded in his efforts to bring not only common men but also nobles and courtiers into his fold and was to see the influence of these nobles help to change even the emperor's attitude.

But Ahmad had now become physically weak and felt that the hour of his death was drawing near, so he took the king's permission to leave for Sirhind. Soon thereafter he died in 1624 at the age of 63 and was buried in Sirhind.

Shaykh Ahmad is called *Mujaddid,* because his mission was to purify Islam of all those anti-Islamic practices which, on account of indigenous influences, had become prevalent among Indian Muslims. Indeed, Akbar's liberal religious policy had aggravated the situation to the point where people did not hesitate to indulge in un-Islamic activities. That was why Shaykh Ahmad felt it necessary to take bold steps to purge society of these elements. . His method of bringing about a religious renaissance was very far-sighted and he had a remarkable capacity for organization To achieve his ends, he imparted training to his disciples and then sent them off to different regions to propagate the true teachings of Islam

One great contribution he made to *tasawwu*f lay in the field of its theology. His goal was to bring *tasawwuf* more in line with the teachings of the Quran and Hadith, for in his times it had come closer to yogic practices and Vedanta philosophy. He therefore admonished people to observe the tenets of Islam as enshrined in the Quran and Hadith. He also strove to harmonize Sufi teachings with the Shariah and his efforts were certainly rewarded. In those days listening to music, dancing and worshipping the saints were common practices in Muslim society, but. Shaykh Ahmad forbade his followers to participate in any such activities. Reforms of this kind were successfully carried out by his disciples

.What is regarded as his most important contribution to *tasawwuf* is his concept of *wahdatush shahood* (unity of consciousness). In his day, under the influence of Vedanta philosophy and Ibn Arabi's doctrines of the oneness of being, the mystics had adopted the concept that God and the universe were, in essence, one and co-eternal, and that the universe was not the manifestation of the attributes of God, but Reality Himself made manifest as the universal consciousness. The world was identified with God. Ibn Arabi held that there was no existence save the existence of God. God was both the Ruler and the ruled, the Creator and created. The world was the result of the manifestation of God. It was not a creation of God. To Ibn Arabi, the mystical union did not amount to 'becoming' one with God, rather it was the realization of a union which already existed.

This is the concept of God in Vedic philosophy. In the Vedic view of life everything was God, and of the same essence. Such a concept was not compatible with the teachings of Islam. According to the scriptures, the world was created by the will of God and was also sustained by God. Man was also created and sustained by this same God. Only God was the Eternal Reality. Everything else was ephemeral. Thus the concept of *wahdatul wajud,* which had become popular among the Sufis, had no basis in the Quran and the Hadith. In Islam, God is One and Indivisible, an Absolute Whole. The Creator and the created are separate. The world exists and it is other than God.

The Quran has this to say:

And call not, besides Allah, on another God. There is no God but Him. Everything (that exists) will perish except Himself. (28:88).

Shaykh Ahmad Sirhindi criticized this theory of *wahdatal wajud.* To Ibn Arabi, God and the world were identical. The Shaykh believed that the world was not one with God, but proceeded from God; that the existence of God was real, while the existence of the world was unreal and imaginary; that the universe was not God, but the Shadow of God. This concept, the Shaykh felt, was entirely in consonance with the unity of God.

He explains his concept by a simile: "The presence of the world is like the presence of the image of an object in a mirror. Thus the presence of the image is not the existence of the object. The object is real, but the image is unreal. The existence of the image is a shadow existence (*wujud zilli*) totally separate from the real existence (*wujud asli*) of the object. In this way the existence of the world is a shadow existence, separate from the real existence of God."

Wahdatush shahud also means unity of vision, that is to say, the experience of union or oneness is related to vision rather than reality. The experience of union does not mean that man becomes God. In reality, the servant will remain the servant forever. After explaining this concept, Shaykh Ahmad concludes: "May God save us from their blasphemous ideas."

Shaykh Ahmad's description of his personal spiritual experience was unparalleled in its great clarity and precision. Khaliq Ahmad Nizami writes: Shaykh Ahmad's clarity of thought invested the world of spiritual experience with a touch of realism which was unique." Drawing on this experience, Shaykh Ahmad put forward his ideas so forcefully that the doctrine of *wahdatush shuhud* was accepted not only by his disciples but also by others who were not associated with the order.

Shaykh Ahmad laid the utmost emphasis on the observance of the Shariah, for, in some other orders, the Shariah had come to be relegated to a secondary place. He also boldly criticized all the innovations which were not compatible with the teachings of the Quran and Hadith. For example, he did not hesitate to oppose Akbar's attempt to evolve a new religion combining the teachings of different religions. In any case, Akbar's endeavours failed even in his own times for, except for a tiny minority, no one was willing to convert to this man-made religion; Akbar's subjects did not even fear his displeasure on account of their recalcitrance.

Shaykh Ahmad succeeded in putting an end to the influence of Din-e-Elahi by approaching the Mughal nobles in Akbar's court. He wrote letters to them encouraging them to take an active part in this matter. Ultimately, Nawb Murtaza Khan and Shaykh Farid succeeded in persuading Jahangir to defend the law of Islam. Aurangzeb, for his part, had great respect for the Naqshbandi saints. In fact, he had received his spiritual instruction from the sons of Shaykh Ahmad.

Shaykh Ahmad believed that a truly faithful Sufi would never transgress the law. He criticized the Ulamas for doing nothing but issuing fatwas (religious decrees), and for taking no pains to effect the internal purification which was necessary for receiving divine inspiration: the mere outward observance of rites and rituals would benefit no one. Shaykh Ahmad, moreover, did not spare those Sufis who indulged in senseless wrangling. The Shaykh and other Naqshbandi saints, as well as disapproving of music and dance to induce ecstasy, did not like the loud utterance of God's name, for when God was as close to us as our jugular vein, what was the point of loud recitation? Shaykh Ahmad writes in one of his letters that "with the Naqshbandi Sufis, guidance and discipline depend upon one's submission to and acknowledgement of the prophetic institution. It has nothing to do with external trappings such as the cap or the genealogy of the Shaykh." (*Maktubat-I-Mujaddid*, book I, letter no. 221)

Here is an excerpt from Shaykh Ahmad's letters published under the title *Maktubat-e-Mujaddid*:

"The mysticism of the Sufis and their relations and inspirations are to be accepted only if they conform to them; otherwise they are to be rejected... An abundance of miracles is not a sign of spiritual superiority... The real miracle of the saintly men is the purification of the souls of their disciples. The soul being immaterial, they have to turn their attention away from materialism. The distinction between a true and a false devotee is that the former adheres strictly to the Shariah, while the latter adheres to his own whims and fancies... Submission to the Prophet's tradition is the real bliss."

Shaykh Ahmad Sirhindi's letters were published in Arabic and the Turkish languages

The Successors of Shaykh Ahmad Sirhindi

IT WAS GOD's special blessing that Shaykh Ahmad Sirhindi's family adopted his religious mission with total zeal and fervour. He was blessed with four sons, Muhammad Sadiq, Muhammad Said, Muhammad Masum and Muhammad Yahya. Not only these able sons but also a number of his grandsons involved themselves in this task of the revival of religion. Khwaja Muhammad Masum (1599-1668) worked so hard for this mission that it is recorded that he had 900,000 disciples. This figure may not be accurate, but there is no doubt about it that he was very popular. A large number of his disciples accompanied him on his Hajj journey in 1657. His spiritual experiences during Hajj were recorded by his son Muhammad Ubaydullah. Khwaja Muhammad Masum worked along the same lines as his father. He would often apply Shaykh Ahmad's teachings to new situations, which is the task of a *mujtahid*.

In his times the Sufis, in order to gain popularity, refrained from criticizing people for their un-Islamic acts. Khwaja Masum in one of his letters writes that such an approach is sinful for Sufis. They are duty-bound to guide the people along the right path. He writes: "The Naqshbandi saints strictly adhere to the ways of the Prophet. Those who refrain from enjoining people to do good and forbid evil have deviated from the path of our order.... Had God approved of non-interference with the people, He would not have sent the prophets." Then he goes on to enumerate a number of great Sufis, including Ibn Arabi, who admonished people for their wrong actions. (*Maktubaat Khwajah Muhammad Masum Sirhindi*).

Khwajah Muhammad Masoom claimed to be the Qayyum of the age. (Qayyum in the Naqshbandi order denotes one who is to shoulder the responsibility of bringing stability, reform and resurgence in his own times.) Shaykh Ahmad had claimed this title for himself and had mentioned it in one of his letters that this role of Qayyum would devolve upon his son Muhammad Masum (*Maktubat Rabbani*, Vol. 3, letter 104). He felt that the reform of contemporary society was his responsibility. This movement was indeed of a missionary nature and mobilized the people not only in India but also abroad. Its promoters appointed their Khalifah and sent them to far-off places to spread their message. The fame of the Naqshabandi saints having reached distant lands, seekers of enlightenment in turn came to India and received their spiritual training under their guidance.

In Afghanistan too this order found fertile soil to work upon. One Maulana Murad (d. 1720), who belonged to Bukhara, came to India to receive spiritual training under Khwaja Muhammad Masum. After completing this spiritual course, he went to Damascus. There he found great support, not only of the people but also of the king. A number of colleges were established there by Maulana Murad's disciples.

In later times in the eighteenth and nineteenth centuries, the Naqshbandi order gained so many converts that it was able to exert a great influence in the intellectual field and also improve its own internal organization. Here are a few more prominent names. Shah Waliullah (1703-1762) Mirza Mazhar Jani-Janan (1700-1781) Shah Abdul Aziz (1746-1824) Sayyed Ahmad Shahid (1786-1831) Shah Ghulam Ali (1743-1824) and Maulana Khalid Kurdi (b. 1776).

Shah Waliullah made it his mission to work for the moral and spiritual regeneration of Muslim society and succeeded in bringing about an intellectual renaissance. Like Shaykh Ahmad Sirhindi, Shah Wahiullah considered Islam to be a complete code of life, offering guidance at both individual and social levels. Feeling that no one could realize his potential unless he developed faith in God, he believed that Islam provided the best opportunity for man's self-realization. He believed that if man received the right guidance, his spiritual evolution went on forever. Death to him was only a turning point, and not the end of the journey. He developed a comprehensive philosophy of the growth of the human soul through mystical experiences.

In the history of Naqshbandi, Shah Waliullah, being an authority on Hadith and *tafsir*, made the greatest academic contribution. His most valued book, *Hujjat Allah al Balighah*, is widely read in Arab countries. It has been translated in part and also in its entirety into several languages, including French. Despite great opposition, Shah Waliullah also translated the Quran into Persian. This was a very great service on his part. In India Persian was the language of educated Muslims and non-Muslims alike and they benefited greatly from this translation. His son, Shah Rafiuddin, a religious scholar, also translated the Quran into Urdu to bring it within the reach of the common man.

Mirza Mazhar Jan-i-Janan engaged in activities which were confined solely to spiritual spheres, unlike Shah Waliullah and his family, who were involved in diverse activities—academic, spiritual and political. Mirza Mazhar Jan-I-Janan had a number of Afghan disciples. He wanted to spread his mission to the non-Muslims as well. Perhaps to bring them closer, he declared that the Vedas were a revealed book.

Shah Ghulam Ali was Mirza Mazhar's chief disciple. His fame had spread far and wide. People from Abyssinia, Syria, Asia Minor and Afghanistan came to him for their spiritual regeneration.

Khalid Kurdi of Damascus, a notable disciple of Shah Ghular Ali, also played an important role in the spiritual life in his country.

The Naqshbandi order had become so popular in Turkey that about 52 Takiyyas (Durgahs) were founded in Istanbul alone. The Naqshbandis made the madrasa and the masjid their centres. For instance, Madrasa Al-Abbasiyya was an active centre of Naqshbandi activity in Baghdad.

The revival of Naqshbandi in Turkey, Afghanistan, central Asia and in many other places besides India shows the success of the efforts made by the order to bring about the spiritual regeneration of people in almost every part of the world.

Firdausi Order

THE FIRDAUSI ORDER originated with Saifuddin Bakharzi, who was Najmuddin Kubra's disciple. Najmuddin Kubra was a disciple of Abu Najib. He was called by his *pir* 'the Shaykh of Paradise'. Hence he came to be known as Firdawsi (Paradise). Najmuddin was seventh in line of succession from Junayd Baghdadi. He died in 1221 A.D. Shaykh Nizamuddin Awliya tells us of Bakharzi's conversion to Sufism. According to a tradition of Shaykh Nizamuddin, Shaykh Bakharzi in his youth even went to the extent of condemning the Sufis publicly in his lectures. Once Shaykh Bakharzi was delivering a lecture, which was full of venom against Sufism. This was attended by Shaykh Najmuddin Kubra, who patiently heard him out. While leaving, the Shaykh asked, 'Where is that Sufi?" pointing towards Bakharzi. Bakharzi then came so heavily under the influence of Shaykh Najmuddin Kubra that, there and then, he made an about-face and became his disciple. After giving him spiritual training, Shaykh Najmuddin sent him to Bukhara. He died in 1260.

He had already sent one of his disciples, Khwaja Badruddin

of Samarqand, to settle in Delhi in order to propagate the spiritual message in India. He arrived at a time when Khwaja Qutbuddin Bakhtiar Kaki had already settled there. Descended from the same ancestor as that of Khawaja Abdul Qadir Jilani, although through a different line, Khwaja Badruddin became the founder of the order in India, where he had good relations with the Chishti Sufis.

This was in the time of Shaykh Nizamuddin Awliya. Both would visit one another and exchange their ideas. Khwaja Badruddin was also very fond of *sama*, so he often came to Shaykh Nizamuddin and participated in *sama* gatherings. He had become very popular and had large number of followers. He resided in Delhi for several decades and lived to a ripe old age. Khwaja Ruknuddin and Khawaja Najibuddin were his Khalifas. Leading the very quiet life of an ascetic, Najibuddin Firdausi was not personally very popular, and it was his disciples who spread his message far and wide. One of his disciples, Fariduddin, compiled a book on *fiqh* called *Fatawa Tatarkhania*, named after Tatar Khan, a nobleman associated with the court of Sultan Firoz Shah Tughlaq. Tatar Khan was a great patron of learning and gave his support to the scholars.

Shaykh Sharfuddin Ahmad Yahya Munayri was the best known disciple of this order. He came from Bihar, his ancestors having settled there in the 13th century. He was born in July 1263, and received the traditional education, which included a study of grammar and language. At that time he had not received any religious education, an omission which he often regretted. When he was about 15 years old, he met Shaykh Sharfuddin Abu Tawwama. His coming into contact with so great a religious scholar was a God-sent opportunity for him.

The Shaykh was originally from Bukhara where he had received a proper religious education. Leaving Bukhara, he had gone on to Delhi, which was then ruled by Sultan Balban. It seems that the local ulama were jealous of him because of his popularity, but for Ahmed, the visit of a religious scholar of the calibre of Abu Tawwama was indeed a great blessing of God. He kept company with Abu Tawwama and even took to living with his family in order to receive religious education from him.

Ahmed passed through Munyar on his way to Sunargaon in Bengal. And very soon Sunargaon became a centre of Islamic learning. A great number of people came to receive religious education from him. Shaykh Yahya died in July 1291. After the teacher's death, Ahmad went back to Munyar, then after staying there for some time, he went to Delhi to visit Shaykh Nizamuddin Awliya. After some time he went to Panipat and met Abu Ali Qalandar. But the latter was perpetually in a state of religious ecstasy, and was therefore unable to become his teacher. Then he came into contact with Shaykh Najibuddin Firdausi.

People started thronging to his side. One of his devotees, Maulana Nizam Madni, built a *khanqah* for him in Munyar. Subsequently, Sultan Mohd bin Tughlaq had a great *khanqah* built for the Shaykh and assigned him some land to provide for its needs. This *khanqah* became a meeting place for the common man as well as for religious scholars and Sufis.

A great scholar, he made a profound study of theological and mystical subjects and was very capable of discussing theological as well as spiritual issues. He also wrote books which are regarded as great contributions to Sufism, and when lecturing, in illustration of his points he often used anecdotes

In one of his letters he advised Sultan Firoz to be impartial in dispensing justice, for justice was an attribute of God. Referring to a hadith of the Prophet, he advised his followers that an hour spent in pursuing justice was far superior to forty years of worship (*Maktubat* Shaykh Sharfuddin Yahya Munayri). Shaykh Sharfuddin died in January 1381.

Shaykh Sharfuddin held the view that a Sufi must be merciful and generous to others. He should feed others, even if he had to go hungry himself. He could make do with the minimum of clothes in order to clothe others and he should patiently suffer any cruelty or injustice meted out to him. And he should never retaliate when provoked. He should rather return blessings for abuses. He held that a true Sufi must be sympathetic to everyone, just as the sun shines on enemies and friends alike.

A Sufi must have no attachment with the world and, moreover, should entertain no feelings of self-righteousness. He should be very modest and humble. He believed that humility was essential to the achievement of success in the Sufi path. He taught his followers to assist their fellow men wholeheartedly. He said that acts of kindness and assistance given to the needy were more meritorious in nature than even prayers and fasting. Even prophets of God had gone out of their way to help people in need. Although he was an ascetic and did not believe in establishing contacts with the rulers or others in authority, when it came to helping people in need, he would send letters of recommendation to officials, if he thought that his letters could alleviate their sufferings. He often narrated the tradition of the Prophet that a Muslim was one from whose hands and tongue people were safe.

He even went to the extent of saying that the heart of a sincere Muslim was the home of God. One who broke a Muslim's heart destroyed the house of God. The Shaykh believed that the *nafs* (ego) was the real source of all evil. So Muslims were duty bound to wage a war against the baser parts of human nature. He added that the real war was to be waged not against non-Muslims but against the heretical *nafs* (ego).

Shaykh Sharfuddin believed in ascetic exercises for the development of the spiritual self. He said that the performance of these exercises endowed devotees with supernatural powers, which enabled them to receive divine inspiration. He explained in one of his letters that *tajrid* (solitude) meant complete severance from all worldly things, and that it entailed giving away everything one possessed. He explained *tajrid*, or renunciation, as a breaking away from oneself. This meant absence of concern for the future and total freedom from all anxiety. He said that there were two aspects of seclusion: one was external separation from the world, and the other was an internal separation in which the heart was purified of any thoughts other than those of God.

He believed that the observance of the Shariah was essential for the spiritual life of a *Salik,*, for the teachings enshrined in the shariah were based on divine revelation. Firstly, one had to believe in divine unity and, secondly, in obedience to God.

In his letters we find that he believed in the notion that

the purification of clothes at prayer times had a symbolic meaning: that is, the cleansing of the human heart of the impurities of human weaknesses. And this is what was highlighted in the path of the *tariqa*. Similarly, the performance of ablutions before prayers denoted that one should remain in a permanent state of cleanliness. Facing the *qibla* at prayer times amounted to directing prayers from the heart to God. So he felt that the *Shariah* and *tariqa* were complementary to one another. He believed that it was religion which guided the spiritual journey from this material world to the celestial world. To him, the *Shariah* and *haqiqa* were essential concomitants of the spiritual life: the *Shariah* was the body and the *tariqa* was the soul. Although the higher stages in this journey can be made only by God's grace, God's grace can be received only by obeying the *Sunnah* laid down by the Prophet Muhammad.

He condemned those misguided Sufis who believed that, having been attentive to God, there was no need to say their prayers once they had reached the goal they had set their hearts on. The Shaykh made it clear that that was the path of Satan, who had refused to prostrate himself before Adam. He thought that the Sufi who had realized God was superior to a religious scholar who only had bookish knowledge. The Sufis had discovered the truth through hard struggle and were thus superior. So far as the worldly Ulama were concerned, they had to be shunned like the devil, for they had taken the place of the devil in misguiding the people.

Then the Shaykh held it very important that the disciples opt for a perfect guide to help them along their spiritual path. For the absence of a guide would leave them directionless and they would go astray. The spiritual journey could not be undertaken without the guidance of an experienced teacher. It took a true guide to lead them along the right path towards God realization.

Inspired by the ideas of Maulana Jalaluddin Rumi, Iraqi and Fariduddin Attar, Shaykh Sharufuddin believed in *wahdatal wajud*. He said that the *tawhid* of the *tariqa* was the highest state of the pursuit of the truth, (*Manaqibul Asfiya*, p. 336-337). To him *tawhid* or *wahdatul wajud* was the final stage in the Sufi journey to the world of Unity, where he became the recipient of the divine light. He absorbed the particles of this divine light. It did not make him God. He did not cease to exist. It was just like looking through a mirror. Neither did the mirror cease to exist. The state of receiving divine energy through the vision was called by the Sufis absorption in monotheism. Here, above all, the recipient was in need of divine grace

The Successors of Shaykh Sharfuddin

THE SHAYKH HAD a great following of disciples numbering more than 100,000. Of these, Shaykh Muzaffar, Malikzada Fazluddin and Maulana Nizamuddin were the more prominent. Shaykh Muzaffar, whose ancestors had come from Balkh, received his education in Delhi and also taught in a seminary founded by Sultan Tughlaq. After some time he returned to Bihar. There he became Shaykh Sharfuddin's disciple. The Shaykh put him through rigorous spiritual exercises. He would undergo an ascetic regimen in the *khanqah*, until he was reduced to mere skin and bones. The Shaykh was so impressed by his spiritual achievements that he was excused from performing these exercises. Then he left the *khanqah*, but he always remained in touch with the Shaykh. Their communication was often through letters.

After the death of Shaykh Sharfuddin, Shaykh Muzaffar set out for Makkah to perform Hajj and lived there till his last breath.

Qazi Shamshuddin was another important disciple of Shaykh Sharfuddin. Being an administrator in Chausa (Bihar) he did not have time to attend the assemblies of his Shaykh. Therefore, the Shaykh used to write to him letters. These letters, running into hundreds, cover a wide range of topics discussed by Sufis. These were *tawhid, tawba* (repentance) miracles, revelation, inspiration, the Shariah, *tariqa, haqiqa, zikr*, etc. These letters were copied by other Sufis under training, who, in turn, spread further the message contained in them. Thus the Sufi philosophy very soon spread all over north India.

There were several publications of Shaykh Sharfuddin's letters in the 19th and 20th century. These letters clearly show his preference for an ascetic life. He even criticized one of his disciples, Maulana Sadruddin, for having accepted the post of a deputy Qazi. To him it was nothing but a waste of time.

His discourses were collected by a disciple under the title *Ma'danul Ma'ani*. In these, he discussed the religious and spiritual duties of Islam and the social and ethical responsibilities of Muslims in relation to the verses of the Quran, the traditions of the Prophet and the sayings of the Sufis.

He had a large number of disciples. A number of *khanqahs* were built in Bihar and Bengal. The spiritual teachings embodied in his letters spread almost all over the subcontinent within a short period of time.

Teachings

AS WE LEARN from the letters of Shaykh Sharfuddin Yahya Muneri the first stage for the Salik is Taubah (repentance). Taubah, he explains consists of a sincere resolution to abstain from sins. It is Taubah which turns man into a true believer.

The Shaykh believed that the spiritual path was beset with thorns, therefore a Teacher/Guide was required to traverse it. The Master imposes a three fold discipline on the Salik. This discipline consists of: 1. Service of the world for a year 2. Service of God for a year. 3. Watching the heart for a year.

The Perfect Guide is supposed to have four equalifications:

1. Complete devotion to God

2. Capacity to receive truths direct from God without any intermediary.

3. Nearness to God.

4. Acquisition of Knowledge from God without any intermediary.

This stage can be attained by someone whose heart is fully purified from all kinds of worldly desires. Such a person is able to fix his attention on God, the source of all knowledge. If a disciple wants to benefit from the spirituality of his master, he must fully surrender himself to his Teacher. The teacher is the Channel of the transmission of blessing and mercy from heaven to earth.

The disciple can receive divine blessing only when he is able to fully detach himself from the world. He has to practice absorption. A disciple has to lose himself in the Teacher. He has to cast off all his desires and follow the Teacher in true submission. It is by fully submitting to his Teacher that he submits fully to his Lord. As we learn from the Hadith, "One who obeys the Messenger obeys God."

In one of his letters dealing with purification he writes:

It is purity which makes man respectable. Purity is the storehouse of all virtues. Islam is based on purity. There are three stages of purity. 1. The purity of the body, the garment and food 2. The Purity of the senses, that is, abstinenance from sins and transgressions 3. The Purity of the heart. It consists of renunciation of all evil qualities like envy and malice.

The essence of tauba is to turn from impurity to purity. The purity of the heart is the final stage in this spiritual journey. God becomes his constant guardian. He starts living under His ever-watchful eye.

In one of his letters he has explained the difference between shariah and Tariqa. The Shariah purifies the heart, cleanses it of all moral evils like hypocrisy, avarice, greed and so on. Shariah or religion deals with external conduct and bodily purification, while the Tariqa or path deals with the inner purification. The one is like matter or the body. The other is like the spirit or the soul (letter 25 and 26).

In letter 28 he writes that after morning prayer, the twilight should be spent in zikr, the remembrance of God, reciting the Divine names and in repentance. If possible, one should try to spend this time in the company of his Master. Similarly he should spent sometime in the remembrance of God and in introspection, reviewing the gains and losses in terms of spirituality during the day. While going to bed one should continue recitations and one should try to get up in the latter part of the night before twilight for performing zikr.

What he considers of utmost importance in this spiritual path is the motive of the disciple. The motive is likened to the life in the body and light to the eyes. As the body without life or the eye without light is useless, similarly the acts of a disciple without a pure motive are as good as mere form. If desire and love of the world predominate in the heart of a man all his acts will be worldly, even acts of worship. If desire and love of heaven predominate in his heart, all his acts will be heavenly, even such acts like eating and sleeping.

Therefore, a disciple must attach all importance to purifying his motive. For this he has to obey the instructions of a Teacher. This is the only way to purify his motives.

In one of his letters the Shaykh tells the signs of a man's love for God.

1. Being given to prayer and seclusion

2. Preferring the Divine Word to human words; the Divine Presence to the sight of man; the service of God to the service of the world; and not grieving for any loss save separation from Him.

3. To him the first stage on the path of seeking God is humility. Someone has aptly said: 'Humility is the messenger from God to man.' He who seeks God will surely find Him. The seeker must get rid of his self-conceit and self-respect with asceticism and purification.

He held knowledge to be most important for purification just as ablution was to prayer. Knowledge was of two kinds, one received from books and the other through inspiration.

The traveller on the divine path has three states. 1. Action 2. Knowledge 3. Love. All these stages can be traversed by the help of a teacher. One who wishes to discover the truth must serve a teacher. The experienced teacher teaches the disciple according to his capacity.

To attain any gain in this spiritual path service is regarded as an essential duty for the disciple. The gains of service are superior to those of worship. It is a killer of ego. It breeds humility and good manner.

It destroys pride, impurity and illumines the soul. The sages have held that there are a number of ways to reach God, but the best and the shortest in that of service.

Renunciation of the world is necessary for the service of the Lord. The heart is one, it cannot be focused on two things at the same time—the world and the Lord. The final stage in renunciation consists of complete indifference to the world. This state can be accomplished only with the help of the Divine Grace.

The expulsion of worldly desires from the mind is most difficult task. It is only Divine grace which can enable one to drive out worldly desires from the mind. The separation of the heart from worldly cravings is superior to the separation of the body from worldly objects. Renunciation is the basis of all virtues and is the first condition of discipleship. Renunciation can be divided into three kinds. 1. Abstinence from what is forbidden by the scriptures. 2. Abstinence from over-indulgence in lawful pleasures. 3. renunciation of that which separates man from God. This is the highest stage of renunciation (letter 75)

Purity of body as well as of mind is necessary at all times. Purity of body alone is not sufficient. Both purity of mind and body are required for the Divine attraction to uplift the seeker to the highest stage. The gate to this path is knowledge and wisdom. Knowledge is the key to all virtues, as ignorance is the key to all vices. It is therefore obligatory for the seeker to seek knowledge and the company of the wise. True knowledge is that which leads to God. False knowledge is that which leads to wealth and world positions.'

Real Knowledge comes from the soul, and a true knower is he in whom lies the original and final knowledge. The purer the soul, the deeper and more subtle its realization of the Divine (letter 6).

The Sufi Concept of Meditation

Introduction: What Is Meditation?

THE WORD MEDITATION is one of those common words, which we encounter very often in everyday speech and rarely think of all the nuances of meaning, which it may contain. The context in which it is going to be discussed here is religious and the religion discussed is Islam. Islam like Judaism and Christianity is a monotheistic religion, but there are other religions too, where meditation is an accepted practice, that might be described as polytheistic for example Hinduism or non-theistic like Jainism. Therefore it is necessary to construct such a definition of meditation that would do justice to a whole range of experiences taking place within different religious frames.

Meditation encompasses an extremely broad range of practices connected to many of the world's religious and philosophical traditions. It generally includes refraining from random, disturbing thoughts and fantasies, and aims at calming and focusing of the mind on some specific object. Sometimes it requires a strenuous effort while at other times it is entirely an effortless activity experienced as just happening. Different practices involve focusing one's attention differently. A variety of positions and postures might be involved for example sitting cross-legged, standing, lying down, kneeling and walking. At times certain devices like prayer beads (Islamic *tasbih* and Roman Catholic *rosary* for example), symbolic representations of the deity, singing and dancing or even consumption of narcotic substances might be used to induce the right frame of mind.

The stated purpose of meditation varies almost as much as the practices. It has been seen as a means of gaining experiential (practical) insight into the nature of reality both in the case of religious and spiritually inclined persons as well as those who profess to follow no religion at all. It is also perceived as a very effective way of drawing closer or even becoming one with the Ultimate Reality irrespective of what one might think it to be. Meditation thus requires and therefore develops: power of concentration, greater awareness, self-discipline and calmness of mind.

In the *samadhi* or *shamatha*, or concentrative techniques of meditation, the mind is kept closely focused on a particular word, image, sound, person or idea. This form of meditation is found in Buddhist and Hindu traditions including Yoga as well as in medieval Christianity, Jewish *Kabala* (mystical trend in Judaism) and some practices of Sufis. Related to this method is a silent repetition in the mind of a memorised passage from the scripture or a particular word. *Dhikr* or remembrance of God would fall into this category. So would *simran* and *nam japna* of Sikhism.

In *vipassana* (insight, or seeing things as they are) type of meditation the mind is trained to notice each perception or thought that passes through it, but without "stopping" on anyone. This is a characteristic form of meditation in Buddhism, especially Theravada and Zen but does not seem to play much role in Islam.

In *annapuna* meditation attention is focused on breath. The Sufis used this practice as well, and it is often alleged that it was adopted under the influence of Indian, both Hindu and Buddhist, traditions.

As the concept and practice of meditation are assumed here to have as its inspiration religious and spiritually charged circumstances it is important to shortly define the term religion itself. Religion can simply be described as a set of systems, which aims at bringing its follower to the source of Truth. Most of the time religion would have at its centre a scripture, often divinely revealed (ex Quran in Islam). That would be then interpreted through theological writings over a period of time. But a religion also necessarily develops a practical arrangement actually enabling its followers to reach God or whatever other object/objects the religious practice revolves around. It has to have a practical way of worship, certain symbols and ideas, and a body of worshipers - a religious community. This community then allows an individual to integrate and loose himself within it thus partaking in the means and ways the community has of attaining the Reality and salvation.

One of such ways and means is meditation. But as further scrutiny will reveal meditation is very often linked to mysticism. Mysticism is a unique experience, invariably taking place in a religious context. The person experiencing it interprets this experience as an encounter with the ultimate divine reality. Further, this experience seems to be direct and cannot be explained in rational way. It brings about a deep sense of unity and of living on a level of being other than the ordinary.[1]

At times and for some people this experience can be gained in a natural and effortless way without any special endeavour on one's side. Others, it eludes totally. But the human mind longs to belong to the Ultimate and experience It at close quarters. From there arises the need for a mentor, a teacher - Muslim pir or murshid, Hindu or Sikh guru, Hassidic rabbi etc. A charismatic leader gathers around himself his followers and mediates their access to salvation. In certain cases the scriptures can replace the need for a living guru (Guru Granth of Sikhism). Sometimes the tomb of the saint becomes the place of pilgrimage and the saint performs the same functions after death as were ascribed to him during his lifetime mediates and acts as a bridge between the believer and God. This is common both to Sufism as well as some branches of Christianity.

In short, meditation seems to be a way of gaining peep at the ultimate reality through extraordinary experience brought about by it; this phenomenon is found in many religious traditions.

Islamic Mysticism: Tasawwuf

MYSTICAL TREND IN Islam is called *Tasawwuf* and it is an act of devoting oneself to a way of life aiming at achieving a mystical union with God. Broadly, it can be described as an intensification of Islamic faith and practice.[2]

There exist a number of propositions for the derivation of the term Sufi as the followers of Tasawwuf or Sufism are called. Some say that it comes from the Arabic word safa, which means pure. Others think that it refers to suffa (a raised floor or a bench in the Prophet's mosque in Medina, where some virtuous individuals used to sit and spend their time in pious devotion) or even saff (a row, like the rows formed by the believers gathered for a congregational prayer in a mosque). But the most commonly accepted definition refers to the word suf, which means wool. This seems to point to coarse woollen garments worn by the mystics and symbolising their voluntary poverty and renunciation of the world and all its pleasures. Gradually, the term Sufi came to designate a group, who differentiated itself from the others in the community of believers by putting emphasis on certain specific teachings and practices of the Quran and the Sunna. By the 9th century A.C., representatives of this group adopted the term Tasawwuf or Sufism as a designation of their worldview and ideology.

In general, Sufis have always looked upon themselves as true Muslims, who take most seriously God's call to find His presence both in the world spread in front of them and the self. They put stress on the inner life of the being, contemplation of one's actions, spiritual development and cultivation of the soul. On theological level, Sufis speak of God's mercy (rahma), gentleness (halima, r'afa) and majesty (jalal). But at the same time they consider The Truth (Al Haqq[3]) not to be obvious to the uninisiated; rather, the truth is hidden and can be accessed through His help alone. For though Allah is Al Zahir (The Evident) He is also Al Batin (The Hidden), as well as Al Fattah (The Opener).

The Sufis trace the origin of Tasawwuf to the sayings and practice of the Prophet himself. Even before receiving the Divine revelation, the Prophet used to spend days and nights in solitary meditation in the cave of Hira near Mekka. It was on one such an occasion that he saw an apparition in the form of an angel who asked him to recite a verse. The Prophet said he could not read, that he was illiterate (ummi) but after the insistence of the angel he recited after him a sentence, which was the first revelation of the Quran (96: 1-5)[4]. That is why Sufis attach such a great importance to meditation and dhikr[5]. Dhikr and meditation were the forms of Prophet's prayers before his Prophethood.

The Sufis also emphasize the Prophet's self-imposed poverty, contempt of wealth and a luxurious life, as well as his fasts, night vigils and additional prayers. The Companions of the Prophet faithfully followed his footsteps and lived simple lives. The Pious Caliphs refused to indulge themselves even in ordinary comforts in spite of having the wealth of the whole Islamic world at their disposal. They considered the love of wealth as one of the greatest obstacles in the path of their devotion to God.

Like in other branches of Islamic learning, Sufism too believes that the true knowledge is the knowledge of God and it is passed down from a master to a disciple. The master's oral instructions give life to the articles of faith. Thus master's fundamental concern is to shape the character of the disciple and help him in attaining his goal, which is to come near to God and become one with Him. This concept of pir-murid[6] relationship emphasises the personal dimension of the relationship between the Divine and the human.

The Sufi Concept of Meditation (*Dhikr And Muraqaba*)

SUFISM, THE FORM which mysticism has taken in Islam, is not so much a set of doctrines as a mode of thinking and feeling within a specific religious domain. It represents in a way, a reaction against the intellectualism, cold formalism and ritualism of Muslim orthodoxy.

Mysticism has been traced to the Prophet and the times of the Pious Caliphs but it gathered strength during the Umayyad dynasty (660-750 A.C.) and grew further over the centuries. Islam prohibited its adherents from practicing the mortifying austerity and asceticism of the Christian monks and Hindu yogis. But in spite of these religious injunctions, asceticism kept on gaining ground within Islamic community, with large number of pious worshippers seeking to secure salvation through devotional practices (often frowned upon by the orthodoxy), meditation and retirement from the society. The worldliness and absolutism of the Umayyad caliphs and their regime were yet another factor pushing pious men to sever their connections with the obviously corrupting world. Turning away from it they found strength in contemplating the mysteries of God, the soul and the creation.

The early ascetics and their spiritual descendents, the Sufis, usually wore, as already mentioned, the undyed coarse woollen mantles similar to those worn by the Christian ascetics. That is why the term Sufi is usually considered to come from Arabic word suf or wool. Gradually Sufi came to designate a very varied group of individuals who differentiated themselves from others by emphasising certain specific teachings and practices mentioned in the Qur'an and the traditions of the Prophet of Islam.

Though originally Sufism was just a pious mystical trend within Islam with certain individuals being more known than others, there was no attempt to give it any organisational form. But the twelfth century saw a crystallisation of a number of silsilas, or orders. Now certain chains of lineages through which different Sufis could be traced were put in place connecting them with a spiritual hierarchy going back to the Prophet, mostly through' Ali and sometimes through Abu Bakr, giving them legitimacy and enhancing the popular appeal through a firm connection with a charismatic and historical predecessor.[7]

Without going into details of early and subsequent development of Sufi orders[8] (sing. silsila pl. salasil meaning "chain, lineage"; or tariqa pi. taruq meaning "way") it can be safely assumed that the different Sufi orders were and still are founded on a unique system based on the relationship between the master and a disciple, in Arabic murshid (director, mentor) and murid (aspirant). To follow the Sufi path (tariqa) it has always been necessary to accept the authority and guidance of those who have already passed through its various stages (sing. maqam, pi. maqamat). The Sufi masters believe that every man has an inherent ability to achieve a release from the self and obtain a union with God. However, this ability being merely latent, the aspirant cannot attain it by hirilself, without the guidance of a mentor. It is only a mentor that can lead him to the ways of proper meditation so that finally he may acquire an insight into spiritual truth. According to Sufism, m'arifa, which means gnosis, cannot be reached through intellectual exercise but solely through ecstatic states. A celebrated theorist of ethical mysticism, Abu Hamid Muhammad al Ghazzali (d. 1111), who is famous within the mainstream Islam as an authority on fikh (jurisprudence) as well as for his perfectly argued and clearly articulated attacks on the philosophers, writes of his own realization of Truth: "I knew that the complete mystic 'way' includes both intellectual belief and practical activity; the latter consists in getting rid of the obstacles in the self and in stripping off its base characteristics and vicious morals, so that the heart may attain to freedom from what is not God and to constant recollection of Him... It became clear to me, however, that what is most distinctive of mysticism is something which cannot be apprehended by study, but only by immediate experience (dhawq - literally 'tasting'), by ecstasy and by a moral change."[9]

The Sufi who sets out to seek God calls himself a traveller (salik). He advances by slow stages (*maqamat*) along a path (tariqa) towards union with Reality (Fana fil Haqq). This path, according to al-Sarraj (d.988), author of *"Kitab al-Luma' fi 'I-Tasawwuf"*[10], the oldest comprehensive treatise on Sufi teaching, consists of the following seven "stages":

1. Repentance (*tawabah*)
2. Fear of the Lord (*wara*)
3. Renunciation (*zuhd*)
4. Poverty (*faqr*)
5. Patience or endurance (*sabr*)
6. Trust in God (*tawakkul*)
7. Satisfaction/contentment (*rida*)[11]

The book of Sirraj in which the stages were thus

enumerated, was written in Iran in tenth century, much before AI-Ghazalli, during the period when Sufism was first being consolidated as a coherent body of spiritual teachings and thus gives one a comprehensive picture of how the mystical path was in harmony with all aspects of Islamic religious law and doctrine. At the same time the author insists upon a multilevel interpretation of the sacred text (Quran), which corresponds to the different levels of understanding capabilities of listeners.

This notion of degrees of knowledge and nearness to God is one of the fundamental characteristics of the mystical teachings of Sufism in general till today.

Virtually nobody can travel along the path without a guiding mentor or the higher levels of knowledge, understanding and proximity to God would elude him forever. So the stages are inherent part of the path and define the ascetic and ethical discipline of the Sufi. By strictly adhering to the above seven stages, the salik is blessed with ten states (sing. hal, pl. ahwal) meditation (*muraqaba*), nearness (*qurb*), love (*mahabba*), fear (*khawt*), hope (*rija*), longing (*shauq*), intimacy (*uns*), tranquillity (*itminan*), contemplation (*mushahada*), and certainty (*yaqin*)[12]; all with God as the referent (object). While the stages themselves can be arrived at and achieved through one's own effort, under the guidance of a mentor, the 'states' are spiritual feelings and dispositions over which a man has no control and are a gift from God. Also, as 'states' are divine gifts they can take many forms and colours and are often beyond description.

A Sufi's "path" is not traversed until the aspirant has passed all the "stages", achieving perfection in preceding one before advancing to the next, and also having experienced whatever "states" it pleases God to bestow upon him. Then only is he permanently raised to the higher planes of consciousness, which Sufis call "gnosis" (*marif'at*) and the Truth (haqiqat), where the "seeker" (*talib*) becomes the "knower" or "gnostic" (*arit*), and realise the knowledge of Reality.

The first place in the list of "stages" is occupied by repentance (*tawabah*). Repentance is described as the awakening of the soul from the slumber of heedlessness, so that one feels contrition for past disobedience. To be truly penitent, one must at once abandon sin and firmly resolve that he will never return to wrongdoing in the future. Turning one's back on the vanities of the world, one then has to seek out a teacher, pir-o-murshid, to guide him on the way to perfection.

The second stage which the aspirant must attain and which is, as it were, necessitated by the first, is called wara', which can be translated as "fear of the Lord" for God detests whatever hinders the heart from giving attention to Him. Hakim Sana'i of Ghazna (d.113!), author of *"Hadiqat al-Haqiqa"* ("Garden of Reality") writes:

"If a thing hold you back on the Way, what matter if it be faith or infidelity? Ifit keeps you far from the Friend[13], what matter if the image be foul or fair?"[14]

Fear of the Lord leads to the third stage, zuhd or "detachment". Zahid is one that has renounced the world in order to give oneself to God.

Logically, the next stage or "poverty" follows. Voluntary poverty is the Sufi's pride as it was the pride of the Prophet

("Faqr fakhri" - "Poverty is my pride" states hadith). Strictly speaking, Sufi chooses neither poverty nor wealth: his only preference is for what God sends or bestows.

"Patience" or what the following stage consists of is a virtue, without which the depths of poverty could not be borne. Thus it is said to be the better part of faith if not the whole of it.

"Trust or self-surrender" is an attitude of one who entrusts himself completely to God. It springs from the very fundamental Islamic position and forms a part of its creed (*aqida*). Its roots are in tauhid or belief in One God. Al Ghazali says: "Tawaqul or God reliance is a stage of religion and a state of progress of the believers. Rather it is the highest state of those who are near God... The meaning of God reliance is intellect, shariat and tauhid, the intermingling of three elements in a proportionate manner."[15]

The last stage or rida denotes a condition in which the spiritual traveller is always pleased with whatever providence sends his way. Junaid (d. 910) says: "He is the greatest amongst men who has subordinated his will to that of the Lord and is content with His dealings."[16]

To emphasize that the aim and end of Sufism and its Way is to reach God, the Truth (Al Haqq) and not merely to pass through so many stages and experience so many states let us recall this anecdotel? about Junaid found in *"Tadhkarat ul-auliya"* of Farid ud din Attar (d. 1229).

"For forty successive years Junaid kept awake the whole nights in his devotional practices. Thereupon the pride was born in him that he had reached the spiritual pinnacle. The Divine Voice reprimanded Junaid and said, 'The time has arrived when you should be declared a heretic.' He cried,

'Lord! What is my fault?' The reply came, 'Could there be a greater sin than that 'you' in you still survives (i.e. your ego is not yet dead)?' He sighed and bowed his head in submission saying,' He who attaineth not to the union of the Lord, all his virtues are sins.'"

It might be said that spiritual practice is the core of Sufism and Sufi writers have certainly elaborated upon theories and metaphysical points of view, but it is in meditation, prayer, fasting, and day-to-day practices that we find the life of the mystical path. A great many Sufi writings in fact treat these kinds of practices in great details. IS This is particularly true of the meditative practices associated with the "recollection" (dhikr) of the names of God. Dhikr Allah or remembrance of God refers to invocation of the Divine Name. The Quran often speaks of dhikr as an act of worship: "Remember Me, I will remember you" (2: 152). "Invoke the name of your Lord and devote yourself to Him with an utter devotion" (73:8) and "Remembrance of God is greatest." (29:45)

Dhikr is regarded as the most important element of Sufi meditation. For the Sufis, *dhikr* is a method of spiritual concentration consisting of an invocation of the Divine Name or repetition of a sacred formula under the direction of a spiritual master belonging to a legitimate mystical order with an authentic chain of transmission (*silsila*). The spiritual master or sheikh gives the practitioner the necessary permission to perform dhikr.

The performance of dhikr is essentially a spiritual exercise through which Sufis are able to experience God's presence in every fibre of their very being. it is through dhikr that they achieve fana' or "annihilation" and subside in God for ever (baqa'). Junaid says: "Whosoever repeats the Name of the Lord merges into the Name and the Name merges into the Lord."19 Another Sufi says: "The first stage of dhikr is to forget self, and the last stage is the effacement of the worshipper in the act of worship, and total absorption in the object of worship."20

Dhikr was performed both communally and in seclusion. The former enabled senior Sufi disciples to supervise the progress of their juniors. The dhikr-i-khafi, recollection performed either mentally or in a very low voice, was recommended by the Naqshbandis.21 The Chishtiya22 and Qadriya23 generally performed dhikr-i-jali, which was recited aloud. Both forms of dhikr required control of breath, of inhalation and exhalation. The formulas of dhikr itself differed from one order to another, but generally involved the recitation of various syllables of the kalima (Muslim profession of faith) or one or some of the many names of God, for example: "Glory be to God" (Subhan Allah) or "There is no god but God" (*La illaha lil allah*), with an intense concentration of every mental and physical faculty upon the single word or phrase. The chanting might be spoken or silent - just repeated in the mind without uttering the words themselves and the Sufis always attached great value to this repetition or litany for it enabled them to enjoy an uninterrupted communion with God.

Sahl ibn Abdullah al Tustari (d.896)24, a noted Sufi of an early period, asked one of his disciples to keep on saying "Allah! Allah!" throughout the day, without any intermission. When the disciple acquired the habit of doing so, Sahl instructed him to repeat the same words during the night, until they came forth from his lips even while he was asleep. Finally the disciple's whole being was absorbed by the thought of Allah.

Dhikr popularised the used of tasbih (rosary), consisting of 99 or 100 beads to facilitated the recitation. Some orders used rosaries of 301 or 1000 beads. The rosary acquired symbolic importance through its use in ceremonies of initiation and other rituals of the orders. It was also a symbol of authority. The rosary of the founder of the branch of the particular order was inherited by his successors, being especially reverenced since it was impregnated with the *baraka* (blessings) of a lifetime's recital of divine names.

Dhikr has a variety of forms, which have been elaborated upon in the Sufi writings: dhikr-ijali, dhikr-i-khafi, habs-i-dam, pas-i-anfas, naf-i-asbat. Breathing exercises, controlling respiration, and adopting specific sitting postures go with dhikr.

Dhikr-i-jali consists of sitting in the usual prayer postures and loudly reciting the word "Allah" from one's left side, and then from one's throat. Repetition of the word "Allah" may grow more and more intense, and louder with each successive breath, repeating being done first from one's right knee and then from the left knee.

Some Sufis fold their legs under them and begin repeating "Allah" (first from their right and then from their left knees). The process goes on and on like this. Thus salik may, seated in the same position, shout the word "Allah" first from left knee, then from the right, then from the left side, and then, finally, in front, still louder.

Some Sufis may be observed sitting with their eyes closed in prayer in a position facing the Kabah, uttering LA; drawing the sound as if from the navel up to the left shoulder; then uttering ILLAHA (the sound rising from the brain). Finally ALLAH is repeated from the left side with lots of energy and stress. These exercises are called dharb (strikes). Dharb is performed from all sides: front, navel, brain, etc.

Dhikr-i-khafi is a practice of remembering God silently. Following phrases "Allahu Samiun" (God is All-Hearing), "Allahu Alimun" (God is All-Knowing) and "Allahu Basirun" (God is All-Seeing) are successively recited with eyes shut and lips closed. Recitation continues with what is described as the tongue of the heart. Each exhalation of breath begins with *La Ilaha,* and each inhalation with *illallah.* The whole process or technique is set up in numerous manuals, frequently difficult to understand without a commentary of an experienced shaikh.

Habs-i-dam is a term standing for "restraining breathing". Holding his breath the Sufi traveller conceives of his heart (*qalb*) as continuously repeating LA ILAHA ILALLAH. With passage of time the practice becomes intensified to the extent that one can repeat the creed several hundred times within the span of one breath.

Pas-i-anfas is a practice where the Sufi concentrates his inward eye on his heart, which he imagines to be engraved with the word "Allah". Furthermore, he imagines that every inhaling of his is producing the sound "Allah" and exhaling, "Hu", making up the phrase: "Allah Hu" (There is God).

The exercises known as mahmuda and nasira focus one's concentration on a part of the body while practicing meditation. Mahmuda implies concentrating on the tip of the nose while in nasira one's concentration is directed towards the middle of the forehead.

Naf-i-asbat or "negation and affirmation" is yet another method of practicing dhikr. The worshipper sits in the posture of prayer facing towards Makkah. He imagines that he is bringing up *LA ILAHA* from his navel, and. then he expels his breath by a jerk in the direction of his right shoulder. He then utters *ILLA ALLAH,* jerking his head towards his heart, as if imprinting these words upon it.

Dhikr was followed by meditation to allow the individual thoughts of Sufis to emerge and envelop them. Generally, a dervish meditated on some particular verse of the Quran and at the same time the image of the pir was recalled to mind.

Muraqaba, the Arabic word for meditation literally means "vigilance" or "awareness".

It is an aspect of contemplation (*tafakkur*), waiting upon a spiritual presence, a permanent state of attentiveness. The Prophet said: "My eye sleeps, but my heart is awake." According to another hadith, he said: "Worship God as though you see Him, for even if you do not see Him, He sees you." Anyone who feels sure that God is always watching over him will devote himself to contemplating God and no evil thoughts will find their way to his heart.

This is how the practices accompanying muraqaba (deep contemplation) are carried out as given in the chapter on "*Dhikr, Muraqabah, Tauhid, Daur* and *Halat*" ("Remembrance, Meditation, Oneness of God, Whirling and Ecstasy") of '*Awariful Ma'arif* '[25] of Shahabuddin Suhrawardi (d. 1234):

"The exercises of muraqibah (fearful contemplation) and of tauhid (the unity of God) are as follows:

(a) On their heels, elbows touching, the dervishes sit in a circle; and simultaneously make slight movements of the head and of the body.

(b) Or they balance themselves slowly right to left, left to right; and incline the body forwards and rearwards.

(c) Or, seated, they begin these motions in measured cadence with a staid countenance, eyes closed, or fixed upon the ground; and continue them on foot."

After that follows the *daur* (rotating dance) accompanied by cries "Ya Allah! Ya Hu". The *halat* (ecstasy) is achieved by the combination of dhikr, muraqaba, daur and putting redhot irons (called gul - the red rose - by the participating dervishes) in their mouths, which however show no wounds next day.

Al Hujweri (d. 1077) author of another Sufi manual *"Kashaf al Mahjub"* ("The Revelation of the Mystery"), writing much before Suhrawardi, says: "When self-will vanishes in this world, contemplation is attained, and when contemplation is firmly established, there is no difference between this world and the next."

In some orders such as Naqshbandi, muraqaba or meditation begins with the repetition of *"Allahu hadiri"* (God is present before me), *"Allahu naziri"* (God sees me), *"Allahu mai"* (God is with me). God's name may be recited aloud or silently, mentally, as one pleases. Then the worshipper mediates upon some verses of the Quran. The following verses are most often meditated upon:

"He is First. He is Last. He is Manifest, Hidden, and The One Who Knows All Things." (57:3)

"He is with you wherever you may be." (57:4)

"We are closer to man than his jugular vein." (50: 15)

"In whichever direction you turn, there is the face of God." (2:109)

"God encompasses all things." (4:125)

"All that is on earth shall pass away, but the face of the Lord shall abide, suffused with brilliance, majesty and glory." (55:26-27)

Thus meditation means forgetting all else besides God and is an intense remembrance of Him. Those who have undergone a rigorous training under a guidance of a spiritual mentor may achieve this even when not in their teacher's presence. But though all these practices set Sufis apart from the body of the community, they were always very much an integral part of it and played a major role in shaping the popular face of Islam. In general, the Sufis have always looked upon themselves as Muslims who take very seriously God's call to perceive His presence both in the world and the self. They tend to put more stress on looking inward then outward, on contemplation over action, spiritual exercise and development of the self over dry legalism, and cultivation of the soul over social, worldly interaction with people. Sufism considered itself, and does so today too, a science of how to attain a direct knowledge of God and a personal experience of the Divine.

The aim of meditation in Sufism is to activate spirituality. As the Sufis believe that the heart is the centre of spirituality, therefore it is the heart that needs to be activated by turning to practice of meditation. Once the heart is activated a Sufi can reach his goal.

As already mentioned above, *dhikr* may take a very

vivacious and animated mode leading to foot play (daur, raqs) and dancing, accompanied by chant, which might change to almost singing. The Sufi literature often talks of yet another specifically Sufi practice facilitating direct approach to God by activating the heart. It is called sarna' or "listening to music". Sarna' is considered by the Sufis a very effective and powerful technique of achieving the longed for nearness and knowledge of God. Etymologically it is derived from an Arabic verb sarnia, which means a "hearing" or "audition". The word itself does not occur in the Quran in this meaning, but in classical Arabic it meant "a singing or musical performance".

Certain theologians hold that listening to instrumental music is permissible as long as its aim is not merely to amuse oneself, and under-condition that it does not induce sinful thoughts. The lawfulness of music, and connected with it, singing and dancing, have been a subject of long controversy within Islam. Importance was attached to this question when sarna' was adopted as a spiritual exercise and "as a means of revelation attained through ecstasy" by the Sufi circles in the late second or early third century Hijra (9th or 10th A.C.). Thus it was in Sufism that sarna' acquired its technical meaning of listening to music, singing, chanting and rhythmical recitation meant to produce religious emotions and ecstasy (wajd) of knowing God most directly.

All the manuals of Sufism starting with the earliest ones usually have a chapter on sarna' or "audition". As it was a controversial subject, usually they try to justify its use and explain its role in reaching God. Abu Bakr al-Kalabadhi (d. 988) writes in *"Kitab al-Ta'arruflimadhhab ahl al-tasawwuf26:*

"Audition is a resting after the fatigue of the (spiritual) moment, and a recreation for those who experience (spiritual) states, as well as a means of awakening the consciences of those who busy themselves with other things... I heard Abu's-Qasim ai-Baghdadi say: 'Audition is of two kinds. One class of man listens to discourse, and derives therefrom an admonition: such a man listens discriminately and with his heart (as the seat of the intellect) present. The other class listens to music (melody), which is the food of the spirit: and when the spirit obtains its food, it attains its proper station, and turns aside from the government of the body; and then there appears in the listener a commotion and a movement.' AI-Junaid said: 'The mercy (of God) descends upon the poor man on three occasions: when he is eating, for he only eats when he is in need to do so; when he speaks, for he only speaks when he is compelled; and during audition, for he only listens in a state of ecstasy.'"

Like all the other Sufi practices sarna' too is performed under leadership of the sheikh or the teacher, who initiates and ends it with the recitation of Fatiha or the opening chapter of the Quran[27] and controls its every stage as well as duration. Very often it is performed on a Thursday evening and today's qawalli recitals at the shrines of the saints are a continuation of the same traditional practice. It must be remembered that all Persian and Urdu poetry including mystical is intended to be chanted, either to a regular tune or in free musical improvisation. The best performers (of the contemporary: late Nusrat Fateh Ali Khan, Abida Parveen) combine a formal chant with occasional outbursts of improvisation stirring themselves and their listeners to an ecstatic state. In Iran *"Masnavi"* of

Maulana Rumi is often used on such occasions and in the Indian subcontinent, poetry of Amir Khusraw, Bhule Shah (who wrote in Punjabi), Shah Latif (writing in Sindhi) as well as others.

Conclusion

SUFISM CONCEIVES OF itself as a mystical quest for the Truth and all its practices serve this end. The journey along the Path to the One is an arduous one and requires many resources. Meditation in the form of dhikr or remembering God and rnuraqabba or contemplation of mystery of Being and Creation are but devices to help along the Way. But ultimately it is Allah who in an act of grace unveils Himself to the traveller and no spiritual exercise can even attempt to equal His compassion. "A saint saw Junaid after his death in a dream and asked him how God dealt with him. He said, 'He forgave me out of His mercy and not due to my spiritual practices. EXCEPT FOR THE *TWO-RAKA 'T NAMAZ* that I offered at midnight to My Lord, none served any good purpose for me here."[28]

Notes

1. A basic introduction to mysticism might be found in "Mysticism in the World's Religions" by Geoffrey Parrinder, Oneworld Publications, Oxford, 1976; and "Hindu and Muslim Mysticism" R.C. Zaehner, Oneworld, Oxford 1966.
2. For a brief introduction to Islamic faith and practice see "Islam..." by Farida Khanam, Goodword Books, New Delhi, 2001.
3. For the names of God in Islam, see "The Most Beautiful Names of Allah"

by Samira Fayyad Khawaldeh, Goodword Books, New Delhi 2001.

4. For the life of the Prophet Muhammad, see "The Life and Teaching of Prophet Muhammad" by Farida Khanam, Goodword Books, New Delhi, 2004.

5. Dhikr - means literally "remembrance, recollection" and in Islamic context denotes the activity of repeating God's names.

6. For an exposition on Sufi master-disciple relationship see "Pir-Murid relationship: A Study of the Nizamuddin Dargah" by Desiderio Pinto, Manohar, New Delhi, 1995.

7. For early Sufism and development of Sufi orders see for ex "A History of Sufism in India" Vol. I, S.A.A. Rizvi, Munshiram Manoharlal Publishers Pvt. Ltd., New Delhi, 1978.

8. See for example, "The Sufi Orders in Islam" by J.S.Trimingham, Oxford 1971, or particular entries in the Encyclopedia of Islam, Brill, Leiden, 1961 and after.

9. "The Faith and Practice of Al-Ghazali" tr. W.M. Watt, Oneworld Publications, Oxford, 1953, 1994 pg 56-57; the above book consists of a translation of "Deliverance from Error" ("Al-Munqidh min ad-Dalal"), which is largely autobiographical, and "The Beginning of Guidance" ("Bidayat al-Hidayah") from "The Revival of the Religious Sciences" ("Ihya' 'Ulum ad-Din"). For translation of complete "Ihya' 'Ulum ad-Din" see also "Imam Gazzali's Ihya Ulum-id-Din" tr. Maulana Fazul-ul-Karim, Sind Sagar Academy, Lahore, 1971.

10. Abu Nasr 'Abdallah bin 'Ali al-Sarraj al-Tusi "The Kitab al-Luma' fi 'I-Tasawwuf' ed. R.A.Nicholson, London, 1914 and 1963. The title can be translated as "The Book of Flashes". This book has also been translated into Urdu by Sayyid Asrar Bukhari "Kitab al-Luma'" Lahore: Islamic Book Foundation, 1984.

11. For description of 'stages', with references to al-Sirraj and Sufi writers later than al-Sirraj see for ex "The Persian Sufis" by C.Rice, Ltd., London 1964; S.H.Nasr "Sufi Essays", London 1972; and others.

12. As given by al-Sirraj in his manual mentioned above.

13. "Friend, Protector" (Al Wali) is one of the names of Allah. Also, the Sufis

call themselves and are called "Friends of God" (auliya, sing. wali).

14. Quoted after C. Rice, "The Persian Sufis", London 1964, pg. 41.

15. for quotation, see pg. 235 of Book IV, "Imam Gazzali's Ihya ulum-id-din" tr. Maulana Fazul ul Karim, Lahore 1971. This volume deals with all stages of mystical progress.

16. "Tadhkaratul-Auliya" of Farid ud din Attar, tr. Bankey Bihari, Lahore, 1961, pg. 110.

17. See pg. 102 of the above.

18. al-Sirraj, Kalabadhi, Qushairi, Suhrawardi, Hujwiri - just to mention a few authors of Sufi manuals.

19. See pg. 109 of the above.

20. See: "The Mystics of Islam", R.A.Nicholson, London 1963, pg. 48.

21. Naqshbandi silsila - a Sufi order of Central Asian origins, established by Khwaja Ya'qub Yusufal Hamadani (d. 1140), which flourished in India and produced such figures as Baqi Billa (d. 1565), who brought it to Hindustan; Shaikh Ahmad Sirhindi (d. 1624); Shaikh' Abd al Haqq Dihlavi (d. 1642).

22. Chishti silsila - one of the most popular and influential mystical orders of India, introduced by Khwaja Mu'in al Din Chishti (d. 1236). Nizam ud din Auliya belonged to this order.

23. Qadri silsila - order named after' Abd al Qadir al Jilani (d. 1166), with centers all over the Islamic world.

24. See: "The Kashfal Mahjub" of Al-Hujwiri, ed. R.A.Nicholson, London 1967, pg.139-140 and especially, pg.195-210; and "Tadhkaratul-Auliya" by Fariduddin 'Attar, tr. Bankey Behari, Lahore I 961, pg. 83-84.

25. "The 'Awarifu'l ma'arif' by Shaikh Shahab ud din 'Umar bin Muhammad Suhrawardi, tr. H.W.Clarke, 1891, reprinted by Taj Company, Delhi, 1984; pg 293 and following pages.

26. Tr. by AJ.Arberry as "The Doctrine of The Sufis", Delhi, 1994 reprint of 1935 edition; quotations are from the Chapter LXXV "Of Audition" pg. 163-165.

27. see chapter "The Dance of the Sarna'" pg.297-298, in "The Awariful Ma'arif' of Shahabuddin Suhrawardi in tr. of H.W. Clarke, Delhi, 1984.

28. pg. 114 of "Tadhkaratul Auliya" quoted above.